The Ways of Power

The Ways of Power

Hermeneutics, Ethics, and Social Criticism

Paul Fairfield

 Duquesne University Press
Pittsburgh, Pennsylvania

First paperback edition, May 2004
ISBN 0-8207-0360-5 (pbk)

The Library of Congress has cataloged the hardcover edition as follows:

Fairfield, Paul, 1966–
    The ways of power : hermeneutics, ethics, and social criticism / Paul Fairfield.
        p.   cm.
Includes bibliographical references and index.
    ISBN 0-8207-0333-8 (alk. paper)
    1. Power (Social sciences) 2. Political ethics. I. Title.
    JC330 .F335 2002
    172—dc21   2002003348

∞ Printed on acid-free paper.

Contents

The Ways of Power and the Question of Critique

*T*he dominant schools of modern political morality conceive of a just order as one that secures felicity by reigning in the effects of power and adjudicating conflicts impartially in the lives of the citizenry. Rational agents, fully constituted in their being, capacities, and ends, consent to terms of accommodation that are conducive to mutual happiness, principal among which is the requirement that power in its most conspicuous forms be constrained and legitimated on a consensual basis. While in general terms power is typically and roughly understood in modern discourse as the capacity to elicit compliance by forcible means, the power that chiefly concerns the political thought of modernity is the capacity of the state to compel persons under its authority to comply with the rule of law, and frequently to repress and tyrannize. It is power conceived as the possession of state institutions, and to a lesser extent of religious authority and capital, that preoccupies classical and contemporary liberalism as well as Marxist and socialist discourse. Each of these political moralities is designed to cope with power thus conceived, and each proposes to constitute a just order on the basis of principles established on a firm epistemological, metaphysical, and sometimes scientific foundation.

Within contemporary discourses of power and political morality, many of the premises underlying these standard approaches are being called into question. Among the more problematic assumptions are the juridical conception of power and foundationalist conceptions of practical rationality. If one of the principal aims of a just order is to constrain power in the interest of human freedom and equality, what if the juridical model with its exclusive preoccupation with centralized institutions fails to comprehend the nature of power, the operations of which are ubiquitous, multifarious, and ineluctable in human practices? What if what passes for justice, the common good, or truth itself is a disguised form of power as needful of critique and constraint as political authority? Moreover, what if the dominant political moralities of liberalism, Marxism, and socialism all presuppose an untenable metaphysics and epistemology and are unable in view of this to supply a principled framework of critique that can withstand philosophical examination?

Philosophers have too often posed the question of critique within terms appropriated from the theory of knowledge. How is it possible, it is traditionally asked, for political and ethical judgments to acquire the kind of certainty that we have come to expect in modern philosophical argumentation? How may we provide an objective grounding for the various commitments, practices, and institutions that we defend? Underlying these questions is a certain epistemological anxiety about the truth value of our deepest convictions and the worthiness of our way of life. We are cautioned by the dominant schools of social criticism that unless our practices rest upon incontrovertible foundations they will remain unreflective and unguided. Practices and judgments alike will remain without justification until they are brought under the tutelage of principles whose truth value can be demonstrated with near certainty. Contractarians, Kantian deontologists, and utilitarians have long maintained that the only avenue for political morality consists in the articulation of formal methods, patterned after scientific and mathematical models, for testing or deriving judgments and for safely guaranteeing the truth of our convictions. Such theories assert that principles derived through autonomous reason function as major premises in deductive arguments, the conclusions of which represent well-founded moral knowledge. Principles afford unconditioned insight into the truth about justice and the good and are universal in their application, necessary, impartial, and self-consistent. As rational beings, we are endowed with the capacity to transcend custom, tradition, and contingency to occupy the standpoint of morality or "the moral point of view."

While presupposing much the same epistemological ideal, modern ethical theories are of two kinds. Teleological theories draw attention to the consequences of action while deontological theories assert that what makes a right action right is a feature of the action itself. Deontology in its Kantian form asks us to consider whether the maxim inherent to an action passes a test of universalizability; in its intuitionist forms actions are appraised on the basis of self-evident duties. Teleological theories assert that the sole consideration determining the moral status of an action is the consequences that it produces, most often as they pertain to the balance of utility and disutility. Practical reasoning for consequentialists and deontologists alike is a matter of formally deriving the correct solution to a problem in rule-governed fashion. Employing procedures such as the categorical imperative or the principle of utility, such theories fasten upon the single relevant feature of moral action, typically either its consequences or the motives of the agent. This one overriding consideration alone has moral import, while all the remaining features of human action are regarded as morally uninteresting. Further, formal reasoning requires that we ignore such contingencies as the prevailing attitudes of a particular time and place, local forms of self-understanding and norms passed down through tradition, and so on. For deontologists and consequentialists, moral philosophy is a fundamentally epistemological enterprise dominated by formalist conceptions of rationality. Principles, rules, and decision procedures are the indicators of reliable moral knowledge.

Critics of foundationalism have issued a series of objections in recent years against what they regard as modern moral philosophy's epistemological quest for certainty.[1] Incorporating arguments from thinkers as diverse as Aristotle, G. W. F. Hegel, Friedrich Nietzsche, Martin Heidegger, John Dewey, and numerous others, nonfoundationalists have been dubious about many of the epistemological and metaphysical assumptions underlying much of the moral and political thought of modernity. Two of the more compelling arguments against foundationalist and formalist approaches are noted here briefly since both arguments are presupposed in the study that follows.

First, formalist conceptions of rationality which assimilate ethical to scientific or mathematical reasoning are often criticized for ignoring the essential complexity and ambiguity of our moral lives, and for imposing on them simplistic models of reflection. Allying moral reasoning with scientific investigation, complete with algorithms for deriving solutions to problems concerning justice and the good, requires us to abstract from precisely what must be held in view — layers of complexity and significance and inescapable difficulties and conflicts that characterize human action. In their quest for theoretical simplicity, formalist rationalities focus attention on too narrow an object domain. Deontologists and teleologists award exclusive moral relevance either to the outcomes of an action or to its motive with no possibility of a third alternative. Kantians inquire into the motive of the agent to determine an action's moral status and whether it passes a test of universalizability, without considering the consequences of the act; for consequentialists the operation is reversed. Utilitarians consider the outcome of an action and determine whether the net utility produced exceeds its net disutility as compared with alternative courses of action. These formalist modes of reasoning today serve to promote conditions in which issues of public policy increasingly are articulated in the language of cost-benefit analysis, an operation facilitated by research in the social sciences and employing an array of models for predicting outcomes and deriving net utility. Ordinary capacities of perception and practical judgment are displaced by scientific expertise, while the practice of dialogue is displaced by decision procedures for determining how our moral and political lives may be managed with optimal efficiency. Lost in the quest for technique are qualitative perceptions attentive to the richness and complexity of phenomena and to their significance within a broader fabric of ethical life. The complexity and contextuality of social phenomena, the manner in which practices constitute us as moral agents, the layers of meaning which belong to human action are glossed over in an endeavor to be scientific, while difficult issues of moral perception are reduced to simple affairs of problem solving. Moral philosophy needs a conception of rationality that is mindful of complexity while allowing us to cope with such complexity in a reflective manner. This cannot be achieved until the fascination with technique and the quest for certainty are put aside.

A second criticism directed against mainline theories pertains to the alleged capacity of moral reason to transcend the fray of ordinary dialogue and achieve complete distance from tradition, a project that we increasingly are being urged to abandon. A variety of nonfoundationalist schools have insisted that philosophers take seriously the finitude of reflection. Reason is not a faculty of unconditioned insight which severs all connection with tradition and objectively surveys social reality free of all presuppositions. The Enlightenment conception of ahistorical rationality which, bracketing all preconceptions, identifies first principles as a foundation for reflection and derives conclusions on the basis of rules formulated a priori is a myth which, in the wake of Nietzsche, Heidegger, and others, we can no longer take seriously. These thinkers in particular have demonstrated the futility of the search for ahistorical foundations and the mythical nature of reflection that begins from

scratch or attains an unclouded perception of reality. Epistemological skepticism regarding the capacity of reason to comprehend
phenomena *sub specie aeternitatus* is part and parcel with moral
skepticism about foundations and objective standpoints transcending the realm of practice and tradition. Whether "the moral point
of view" assumes the Kantian form of a transcendental perspective on ethical life, the scientific form of a highest stage in the
development of moral consciousness, or the contractarian form of
a presocial perspective, the standpoint of "morality as such" is no
standpoint at all. Social criticism invariably occurs from a finite
perspective, and the degree of illumination it achieves is limited
by the perspective it occupies. Moral reason must be viewed as
being "always already" under way, as operating from a finite perspective within the realm of practice, language, and tradition.

The view that all forms of reflection are characterized by historical contingency has been taken up in recent decades by critics of
foundationalism generally, yet it has received its most pronounced
emphasis in hermeneutical philosophy. Martin Heidegger and
Hans-Georg Gadamer in particular have placed the themes of history, tradition, language, and human finitude at the center of their
ruminations on everything from ethics to aesthetics to the nature
of understanding. What these and other hermeneutical philosophers
emphasize is that all reflection presupposes prereflective understandings which constitute our inheritance as historical beings.
Reflection is invariably limited by the conditions that make it possible, in particular by a horizon of language and tacit presuppositions not entirely of one's own making.

Hermeneutics adopts an attitude of historical consciousness not
only in interpreting texts distant in time and place, but in our thinking about philosophical matters generally, including our approach
to ethics and politics. We are to remain cognizant of our involvement in tradition rather than continue the Enlightenment project
of leaping out of history or beginning from scratch. This project
presupposes that our relation to history, language, and tradition is

that of subject to object, that if we set out from the proper foundation, identify the proper technique and follow its dictates scrupulously we may transcendentalize our way out of history. It overlooks the essential historicity of human existence — the inevitability of our participation in historical traditions and the rootedness of reflection in finite perspectives. "Historicity," "contingency," and "linguisticality" all refer to human understanding's place within a horizon passed down through tradition and which remains largely presupposed. As historical beings, our consciousness of phenomena — empirical, aesthetic, or ethical — is made possible and limited by the perspectives furnished to us by our history. Hermeneutics urges reflection to become cognizant of its conditions of possibility, to view itself as historically situated, linguistically mediated, and contingent (or as lacking any kind of a priori necessity). Historical consciousness serves as a reminder both of our continuing participation in practices, language, and tradition, and of our having been effected in our consciousness by such participation. It urges us to remain aware of the fact that human understanding has limits which no amount of formal methodology could allow us to transcend.

A measure of hermeneutic or historical consciousness has taken root in a variety of nonfoundationalist approaches to moral and political philosophy. Uniting these approaches is a shared skepticism regarding many of the metaphysical and epistemological assumptions underlying much of the history of the discipline. Metaphysical assumptions concerning everything from the form of the good to theological cosmologies, natural law, human nature, and rational choice are increasingly rejected along with epistemological notions of certainty, self-evidence, and a priori necessity. Authors on both sides of the Atlantic as diverse as Hans-Georg Gadamer, Michel Foucault, Jürgen Habermas, Jean-François Lyotard, Richard Rorty, Alasdair MacIntyre, Bernard Williams, and Michael Walzer are one in rejecting assumptions about moral reason as a timeless source of insight into the truth about justice and the good. In different ways these authors accentuate the rootedness of ethical reasoning in finite conceptual frameworks and the impossibility of transcending them by formalist means.

Also uniting nonfoundationalist approaches is a rejection of the claim that normative theory provides unassailable grounds for social practices. Practices that take root in a lifeworld are sufficiently reflective as to require neither transcendental guarantees nor wholesale justifications of the kind that modern philosophy has often sought to provide. What emerges in the aftermath of foundationalism as the principal question of ethics is how it is possible in view of the finitude of moral reason to appraise critically the practices, traditions, and power relations that constitute the social world to which we belong. How can a discourse rooted in tradition and invested with power adopt a critical posture toward these very conditions? How can the conditions that make reflection possible themselves be subject to critique without generating an impossible circularity?

Philosophers who reject foundationalist epistemology are not relieved thereby of the responsibility of determining how social criticism is possible — in particular, from what perspective it occurs, what principles inform it, and how it is able to articulate a philosophically compelling critique of power. If theorizing need not provide foundations for social practices, it must still inform attempts to critique such practices. However, while social criticism may subject any practice, institution, or norm to rational scrutiny, it may not do so on a wholesale basis since there is no vantage point from which social reality in its entirety could ever be held in view. Criticism occurs from within tradition and is immanent to the realm of human practices. The principles it employs are recovered from this finite perspective and are not transcendental deliverances from the region of metaphysics. These premises entail a return of sorts from the pristine world of metaphysical abstractions and formal technique to the finite world of human practice in all its ambiguity and uncertainty, and with all the complexity and layers of significance that belong to human action. The finite perspective of moral consciousness makes unconditioned insight impossible and our most illuminating descriptions partial. Taking human finitude seriously requires us to accentuate both the immanence of social criticism and the difficulty of securing illumination in evaluative description.

These initial premises are shared not only by hermeneutical philosophers but by nonfoundationalists of several schools. Less widely shared are several further premises of hermeneutics that will be central to my approach to the main problematic of this study: the critique of power in its multifarious operations. The first of these concerns the hermeneutic character of social criticism. The practice of criticism is ultimately inseparable from that of hermeneutic interpretation. Critique is a matter of perceiving and understanding contexts of moral action in light of principles. As a mode of hermeneutic disclosure it, like interpretation generally, is not without conditions of possibility — including language and tradition — and is situated within a particular horizon of inquiry. Interpretive understanding, as it is spoken of by hermeneutics, is a dialogical practice that aims at an overcoming of alienation, a rendering intelligible of phenomena whose meaning is not self-evident.

In taking this view, I defend hermeneutics — in particular Gadamer's philosophical hermeneutics — against the charge leveled against it by critical theorists — in particular Jürgen Habermas — that hermeneutical philosophy's accent upon historicity and finitude entails an absence of critical perspective in reflection upon tradition and the power operative therein. This objection deserves to be taken seriously, and it is to a considerable extent with this problem in mind that I set out to formulate a hermeneutical ethics. This study offers a contribution to the debate between hermeneutics and critical theory as well as the debate in contemporary ethics concerning the nature of practical rationality in the aftermath of foundationalism. I argue that critical reflection not only is possible for hermeneutics but is properly conceived as itself a mode of hermeneutic reflection. It is a practice that uncovers meaning in the same gesture in which it fashions evaluative judgments. In taking this position, I shall bring into unusually close proximity two notions that moral theorists often sharply separate: description and evaluation. Ethical critique is both a descriptive and evaluative mode of utterance, one in which it makes as much sense to speak of interpreting texts — hence uncovering meaning — as of appraising the rightness or wrongness of an action. Appraisal, judgment, and evaluation must be thought together with description, perception, and understanding. These two modes of utterance, while distinguishable in principle, are intimately related in the practice of social criticism.

Another premise of hermeneutics concerns the primacy of dialogue in the practice of interpretation. Ethical critique as a hermeneutic discourse is ultimately inseparable from the practice of conversation, since disclosure occurs in the confrontation of viewpoints. In hermeneutic dialogue, opposing perspectives are drawn into engagement with one another in a common effort to reach an understanding, a practice that allows the confrontation of interpretations and competing descriptions. Moral perceptions are neither presuppositionless nor monological, but are fashioned in practical judgment and tested dialogically.

Hermeneuticists commonly maintain that there are no formal techniques for generating insight in interpretation. I maintain further that no amount of moral theorizing could eliminate the need for imaginative redescription, practical judgment, and dialogue. Social criticism, conceived of hermeneutically, is not a rule-governed procedure. The purpose of theory construction is to fashion principles not as decision procedures but as a framework of concepts that illuminate significance and identify saliences within moral contexts. Recognizing the conditions and limits of reflection precludes all foundationalist and totalizing perspectives that would privilege any particular conception of the good or deem any interpretation as supremely authoritative. Yet it does not preclude moral theory in all possible forms, nor does it compel us to abandon a conception of universal right. A responsible universalism retains an attitude of historical self-consciousness and takes its bearings from within the realm of practice, and specifically from the universal practice of hermeneutic dialogue. The practice of dialogical understanding contains an inherent normative dimension which it is the task of hermeneutical ethics to render explicit. When we identify the ethical implications and conditions of a communicative practice oriented toward mutual understanding, principles of universal right reminiscent of classical liberalism are generated. While this argument bears close methodological resemblance to Habermas's communicative ethics, the moral-political position I defend is more in keeping with the liberal tradition than with Habermas's neomarxist view. Thus, normative theorizing introduces a (modest) measure of adjudication into interpretive conflicts without providing unassailable grounds or formal procedures of interpretation. It refrains from privileging perceptions as definitive insights uniquely bestowing enlightenment.

This investigation constitutes an attempt to think in the interstices of standard dichotomies which increasingly and rightly are falling into disfavor. With Nietzsche I share a suspicion of many of the usual dichotomies of modern thought, particularly those arising within moral and political philosophy. Objectivism or relativism, necessity or contingency, deontology or consequentialism, theory or practice are several of the oppositions that in the aftermath of foundationalism appear to have outlived their usefulness. It was only on the basis of foundationalist assumptions that these dichotomies appeared to have any legitimacy, and rejecting these assumptions entails rejecting the dichotomies to which they gave rise. Recent attempts to develop a nonfoundationalist practical rationality have given rise to new oppositions which must equally be rejected. Frequently it is intimated that if we are serious about abandoning foundationalist and totalizing perspectives we must adopt some form of conservatism, communitarianism, or collective decisionism, or that recognizing the finitude of reflection forces us to abandon theory construction in all forms. However, each of these oppositions may be dispensed with and replaced with a conception of ethical theory that is universalist as well as mindful of the conditions and limits of reflection. My aim is to articulate an historically conscious universalism, one that abandons the perspective of unconditioned objectivity without abandoning universality. An historically conscious universalism introduces an important element of philosophical adjudication into interpretive conflicts without dogmatically privileging any set of interpretations as definitive. Critical reflection uncovers neither objective meanings nor moral facts, but neither is it an affair of unreasoning frivolity. It is a practice that provokes, informs, and illuminates with a claim to philosophical rationality.

Different conceptions of ethical and social criticism have been much debated in recent decades by many of the discontents of foundationalism. Among philosophers committed to rejecting both mainline ethical theories and the oppositions that such theories presuppose, there remains little consensus on the question of what critique is or ought to be.[2] Different critical paradigms have been proposed, from Foucault's method of critical genealogy appropriated from Nietzsche to Habermas's scientific critique of ideology. Along with hermeneutics, both attempt to open a space for critique in the interstices of traditional dichotomies. Both are committed to renouncing foundations without having recourse to a conservative position. Both acknowledge the situatedness of reflection while seeking to uncover and describe many of the subtle workings of power which are often concealed from view and which it is the task of critical reflection to disclose. Their insight into the ways of power and their sharing with hermeneutics a commitment to social criticism that is capable of detecting the effects of power while remaining cognizant of the conditionedness of its discourse causes me to devote the first three chapters to separate discussions of Nietzsche, Foucault, and Habermas. The central questions addressed in these chapters concern the concept of power and the critique of power in the work of these central figures of the continental tradition. If it is not from an ahistorical and totalizing perspective that such critiques proceed, from what standpoint do they speak? What methods or principles inform criticism, and how much confidence can be claimed for its descriptions? More fundamentally, what sort of practice is social criticism, and what is it that we are doing when we engage in it? After providing an overview of these three paradigms of critique, I offer an assessment of each, focusing on their capacity to reconcile our historicity with the need for critical rationality.

Beginning in chapter four, I fashion a hermeneutical conception of the theory and practice of social criticism and apply this in a broadly liberal spirit to relations of power that are often overlooked by the dominant modern paradigm. I characterize this approach as hermeneutical for two reasons. First and most obviously, it takes its fundamental orientation from phenomenological hermeneutics, primarily as represented in the thought of Hans-Georg Gadamer and Paul Ricoeur. Much of my basic orientation is derived from central themes in their work. Second, the approach may be so characterized on account of the centrality of the themes of hermeneutic dialogue and interpretation in the following chapters. If we wish to develop a nonfoundationalist and critical rationality we must begin by recognizing the pervasiveness of interpretation and dialogue in our efforts to appraise the forms of power endemic to modern practices. We must begin to think of moral agents not only as rational but as interpretive and self-interpreting beings continually occupied with understanding both themselves and their lifeworld. We must also begin to think of critique as a central element of this most human of practices. Ethical criticism belongs to the universal practice which is the struggle for illumination and self-understanding, a practice ubiquitous in human existence and central to the task of fashioning a just order.

While many of my initial premises are derived from the works of such figures as Nietzsche, Heidegger, Gadamer, and Ricoeur, a group of thinkers often radical in their opposition to modernity, I consider it important not to fall into the habit occasionally taken up by their adherents of overstating the radicality of our position. My approach parts company with many of the usual metaphysical and epistemological assumptions underlying much of the history of ethics, yet it most definitely does not sever all connection with the legacy of Western metaphysics and epistemology. So long as we take seriously the proposition that normative claims require philosophical justification, it is extremely unlikely that the metaphysical and epistemological tradition in its entirety could ever be completely and unproblematically left behind. Philosophical thinking, including its most radical forms, never severs all connection with tradition. The aim of this study is to give up the quest for moral certainty and objective grounds and to take seriously the need for rationality in moral and political discourse, even if this is not the foundationalist rationality of mainline ethical theories.

ONE

The Will to Power and the Politics of Ressentiment

*I*f it is a principal function of the state to circumscribe the reach of power, to place limits on what Thomas Hobbes identified as the ruling interest of subjectivity, and to do so in the interest of justice, what if the will to justice itself is subordinate in the constitution of the self to the will to power? What if what passes for justice is itself disguised will to power, the ambition of either the strong or the weak to fashion social institutions in their own image, securing whatever advantage they can in an unending and ineluctable contest of self-assertion? What if the will to power is altogether ubiquitous in social reality, its operations detectable in all forms of intersubjectivity, the traces of which may never be removed in the way that modern states dream they might?

Modern political discourse, be it liberal, socialist, or otherwise, invariably seeks to offset the effects of the particular will to power it identifies as posing the most formidable threat to civility. Typically either the state, religious authority, capital, or other centralized institutions are singled out as the main object of critique. Just social arrangements may be secured, a familiar argument runs, once the powerful are held in check by the rule of law and in accordance

with the popular will. That power largely resides within an identifiable and centralized agency, that the popular will is itself
uncorrupted (indeed, on some accounts, incorruptible), and that
its overriding concern lies with securing a condition of optimal
civility are premises implicit to many a political argument. They
are also, in Nietzsche's view, evidently false.

Nietzsche proffered the will to power as an explanatory principle
of extraordinary scope, the precise contours of which are a matter
of dispute. While since Hobbes — or indeed the Greeks — moral
and political philosophers have been amply aware of the instinct
for power and the danger that it poses, Nietzsche's doctrine radic-
alizes the Hobbesian view in positing the will to power not merely
as a psychological disposition which when unchecked gives rise
to violent struggle, but as a multifarious and ubiquitous phenomenon of human existence, one that in light of its pervasiveness in
social ontology could never be effectively subordinated to the will
to justice. Political morality being in essence nothing other than a
mode of physio-psychological expression, it is inconceivable that
the will to justice could supersede the will to power. Social reality
is and cannot but be the playground of this will, each competing
faction anxious to present its own will to power as constitutive of
the good.

The problem this view poses for the modern state is formidable:
if it is the nature of power to be multifarious, decentered, ubiquitous, and commonplace — if, moreover, the will to civility and
justice is itself a guise for the instinct to impose one's will as widely
and in as many forms as possible — the prospect of a social order
effectively reigning in the will to power or deadening its effects
appears unlikely in the extreme. Those of us inclined to regard
Nietzsche's philosophy of power as among the more incisive perspectives on power and its multifarious operations face the challenge of appropriating the insight this view affords while refusing
the unsavory political consequences that, on some readings of
Nietzsche, proceed from that view. The authoritarian implications

of the doctrine of the will to power which many readers of Nietzsche have (not always fairly) noted clearly call for critique and
ultimately rejection, yet it is doubtful that the philosophy of power
that Nietzsche proffers contains the resources needed to provide
a compelling critique of power, including its authoritarian forms.
The argument of this chapter is that while the theory of the will
to power affords a consistently illuminating perspective on much
of social reality, particularly on the realm of politics, Nietzsche's
method of critique and positive doctrine are unable to provide an
altogether adequate critique of power or to afford a compelling
alternative to the particular forms of will to power that Nietzsche
rightly condemns.

The Will to Power

Determining the precise scope of this much-interpreted concept
is a matter of some difficulty owing to ambiguities and inconsis-
tencies in Nietzsche's writings. The will to power is alternatively
described by commentators and by Nietzsche himself as a psychological, moral, political, physiological, scientific/cosmological, ontological, or metaphysical principle. Selective reading may lend
support to any of these interpretations, yet due attention to the larger
frame of Nietzsche's thought decisively rules out interpretations
of this principle as any kind of metaphysical or scientific/cosmo-
logical doctrine intended as a successor to the dogmatic metaphysical systems of the past which Nietzsche rejects with disdain. As
a critic of metaphysics and of much of modern science, it is ex-
traordinarily unlikely that Nietzsche would consider defensible the
notion that reality quite literally is the will to power, especially in
view of Nietzsche's sustained critique of metaphysical notions of
essence, the thing-in-itself, the absolute, and so on. The world, in
his view, does not contain an essential nature any more than does
the being of the subject itself. Nietzsche's occasional references
to the will to power as a metaphysical principle are best understood

metaphorically, his confirmed interest lying not in dogmatic meta-physics but in the human lifeworld.

More plausible than the metaphysical and scientific/cosmologi-cal readings are interpretations that restrict the scope of the will to power to the order of organic life and specifically to human (physio-psychological) existence. Nietzsche's interest in nonhuman organic life being of a highly cursory nature, the doctrine of the will to power is properly limited in scope to the order of individual psy-chology and social ontology. It is a principle that seeks to unify and explain a wide array of human phenomena from instinctual drives to ethical relations to artistic expression. At its basis is an imposition of form. The will to power imposes intelligibility on phenomena, interpreting them with respect to significance and value. Lacking sense and value in themselves, phenomena are given form by the will to power, specifically the form of the inter-preter himself or herself. One's own form is imposed in the inter-pretation of sense and the assessment of value, the phenomenal order thus being the dominion of the interpreting agency in whose image it is organized.

In this consists the fundamental drive in human life, one detect-able throughout a variety of manifestations. A fundamental and universal trait of the human constitution, the will to power is no less the will to intelligibility and order than it is a pervasive psy-chological drive to master and control. Within the order of the physiological and the psychological (a unified order in Nietzsche's account), the will to power is less the enjoyment of feelings at-tending power's attainment than the imposition itself, the discharge of force and the production of effects. In this sense, "life simply *is* will to power";[1] it is an appropriation, an expanding of influence, an overcoming of obstacles, and an increase in dominion ranging from the physical to the intellectual, the political, the moral, and the aesthetic. The complete range of instincts manifests one uni-fied drive beyond all choice and conscious intellection. It under-lies human conduct in general from overt acts of "power seeking" to self-overcoming, aesthetic creation, and philosophical discourse. Particularly evident in ethical and political relations, the will to power also manifests itself in the pursuit of acclaim, influence, friendship and love, and the full range of behaviors and drives that fall within the range of psychological investigation. It is, Nietzsche holds, the instinct for power rather than the pleasure principle of utilitarian psychology that succeeds in unifying and explaining such diverse phenomena as the infliction of suffering, benevolence, the pursuit of excellence or profit, generosity, self-preservation, self-destruction, erotic attachment, and so on. In each instance the driving force behind the action or passion is no mere desire for pleasure or aversion to pain, but a more profound will to discharge one's strength and impose one's form on an expansive field of objects, not least of which is the agent's own being. The affects of pleasure and pain, Nietzsche insists, are mere epiphenomena supervening on human action in a wholly secondary and incidental fashion rather than constituting its principal motive. What the agent ultimately desires is not pleasure and the absence of pain but a condition in which struggle, becoming, and suffering are omnipresent. Utilitarian psychology is, for Nietzsche, the worst of naivetes in remaining at a surface level and refusing to probe the deeper sources of human behavior.

A physio-psychology that descends to the depths uncovers in a sense the very antithesis of the utilitarian self. It reveals a plethora of manifestations of the will to power arranged in rank order. One may imagine a hierarchy of its expressions at the summit of which stands power in its most ascendent and life-affirming forms and at the base of which are its decadent and life-negating manifestations. Each form of the will to power contains a given quantum of power and it is this quantum rather than any qualitative difference that determines its order within the hierarchy, the higher or nobler forms expressing a greater quantum than the lower. Human types, moral values, works of art, and entire cultures are ascending or descending, well-constituted and overflowing with strength or ill-constituted and decadent. At the high end Nietzsche identifies the philosopher (or "the philosopher of the future"), the artist (Goethe as the exemplar), self-overcoming, and the intellectual conscience, each of which constitutes the most human of beings or capacities. Lower on the scale are cravings for success and acclaim, acquisitiveness and liberality, and the multiple forms of ordinary respectability. On the lowest rungs are the morality of the herd, *ressentiment*, physical inhibition, brutality, and the nihilistic religions (principally Christianity). Nietzsche assesses each of these with respect to the quantum of power it contains, each being a manifestation or symptom of the particular will to power underlying it.

Of particular note in Nietzsche's assessment are ethical values, also conceived in hierarchical and quasi-physiological terms. Since Nietzsche recognizes no pure realm of morality or "moral point of view," all conceptions of the good fall within an order of rank. The genetic origin of ethical values determines their place within the hierarchical order. Of the highest rank is the good in its "original" form — the constellation of values that proceeds from the self-affirmation of the powerful and well-constituted individual. The noble individual determines value as a spontaneous act of its nature: ". . . our ideas, our values, our yeas and nays, our ifs and buts, grow out of us with the necessity with which a tree bears fruit — related and each with an affinity to each, and evidence of *one* will, *one* health, *one* soil, *one* sun."[2] In its original form a primordial act of self-affirmation and self-assertion, evaluation belongs no less to the order of the will to power than interpretation — the imposition of form — itself. The attribution of value has its source within the physio-psychological constitution of the individual and is fundamentally an expression of its will to power. It is, accordingly, an instinctive and hence quite involuntary attribution, by no means the inferred conclusion of a practical syllogism. "[T]he greater part of conscious thinking" is, for Nietzsche, ". . . included among instinctive activities." Philosophical thought in general and moral evaluation in particular are symptoms and expressions of "physiological demands for the preservation of a certain type of life."[3] Values are surface phenomena that simultaneously express, conceal, and further the particular will to power that stands beneath them.

Lower grades of humanity express through moral evaluation a will to power of a correspondingly lower order. Self-assertion here gives rise to moralities of a degenerate form, from the communalist and traditionalist "morality of mores" to the decadence moralities of the Judeo-Christian tradition, the categorical imperative, and utilitarianism. Lower-order moralities invariably assume a view of the individual as a function of the herd; the values of altruism, solidarity, and pity are expressions of the weakness that prevails among its numbers. Physio-psychologically, decadence moralities proceed from weakness and inhibition. Egoism here assumes collective form as a survival strategy against the powerful.

Nietzsche's division of moralities into ascending and descending forms again ultimately turns upon quantitative differences in the power of which they are expressions. They are ranked according to the will to power from which they proceed, a noble morality expressing a nature that is robust and well-constituted and a base morality being the expression of impotence. Moral values are conditions of existence for those whose nature they serve, and in the case of the weak and powerless they are strategies of resentment.

Masters and Slaves

The notion of rank order pervades the greater part of Nietzsche's thought, and nowhere more so than in the philosophy of power and morality. Itself an instinct of power, the instinct for rank — which, for Nietzsche, "more than anything else, is a sign of a *high rank*"[4] — belongs to the fundamental constitution of the noble soul. Those of the highest human type seek power in a variety of forms, yet certain tendencies and commonalities are detectable within these forms, first of which is the pathos of distance that elevates and separates itself from that which it judges to be of an inferior order. "Every choice human being strives instinctively for a citadel and a secrecy where he is saved from the crowd, the many, the great majority — where he may forget 'men who are the rule,' being their exception — excepting only the one case in which he is pushed straight to such men by a still stronger instinct, as a seeker after knowledge in the great and exceptional sense" (26). Not solidarity but solitude is the condition of their existence, separation from the mass of humanity for which they feel instinctive disdain. Phenomenologically, such individuals experience themselves as of a higher order than the mass. They assume spontaneously the right to create values yet without legislating the good for others, most especially for those of a lower rank. They determine the good in egoistic fashion yet not in a sense connoting aggressiveness toward those perceived as inferior. Their contempt for the latter is closer to indifference than enmity, and in the normal case does not motivate the infliction of harm. To Nietzsche, seeking power over inferiors is evidence of lower rank. The ignoble type, together with the categories of "bad," "base," and "inferior," is a minor, even trifling, consideration for the will to power of the strong. Master morality is not an expression of hostility or a negation of any sort, but a spontaneous affirmation of self in which those of a lower order do not significantly factor.

The initial affirmation that animates master morality is an affirmation of difference. It is not (or not primarily) domination but autonomy that is sought, separation from and elevation above the mass which would have it fall in line with its collective (and collectivist) values. The morality of the powerful prizes the virtues of solitude, self-discipline, intellectual conscience, honesty, and sympathy, but above all it is individual difference and self-creation that animate the way of life of Nietzsche's highest type. These are fundamentally inward-looking virtues, indicating a certain preoccupation with self and with the projects with which its existence is occupied. This is the inwardness of the creator, the artist, and the philosopher, yet as an affirmation of difference it is not a morality that issues a uniform set of prescriptions binding all persons. Indeed, as Nietzsche writes in *The Anti-Christ*: "The profoundest laws of preservation and growth demand the reverse of this: that each one of us should devise *his own* virtue, *his own* categorical imperative" (11). The life of the powerful and the creative does not conform to a unified model but, in the fashion of the work of art, assumes a variety of forms. Therefore, master morality purposely refrains from prescribing how the noble must conduct themselves and their affairs and restricts their values to a particular human type.[5]

This higher order of beings seek power primarily over themselves rather than other persons, particularly those of a lower order. Typically of an egoistic, inward, and solitary nature, the noble type manifests its will to power by bringing the multifarious and often conflicting elements of its "first" nature into coherence. It imposes form on its instincts, overcomes internal obstacles, and in the course of so doing fashions its own "second" nature. The herd animal it overcomes is the one internal to its nature, the herd without being largely a matter of indifference. In imposing coherence and "style" on its character, the powerful type roots out all elements of mediocrity and redirects instinctual drives in a creative direction. It sublimates affects, rechannelling a given quantum of power in a creative direction and transforming it thereby into a more powerful drive — also a more aesthetic one. Optimally, it "gives style to its character" in the fashion, again, of a work of art, integrating and fashioning disparate elements into a coherent configuration conforming to no set pattern but to the will to power of the agent alone. By integrity or "style" Nietzsche connotes a willed integration of personal traits and passions, a harnessing and a sublimating of impulse rather than any form of repression. Nietzsche's powerful type gives form to its own being not by extirpating the passions but by integrating them into a coherent and willed configuration. The will to truth, for instance, is for Nietzsche sublimated will to power, as are works of art, science, and indeed all of higher culture. Each of these involves a certain "hardness" of self absent from ignoble natures, content as the latter are to anaesthetize robust instincts in exchange for security.

The will to power, then, in its highest manifestation would sooner master itself than others, although imposing its will or personal form upon other individuals may also take place. The caricature of the Nietzschean individual brutalizing everyone it meets has long since been debunked, principally by Walter Kaufmann in his classic study of Nietzsche's thought as well as by more recent scholarship. While the dark side of Nietzsche's philosophy of power should not be soft-pedaled (as Kaufmann, in his enthusiasm, sometimes does and as his critics have rightly pointed out), what must be emphasized is that for Nietzsche's highest type "overcoming," "mastery," "hardness," and "cruelty" are behaviors that are primarily — but not exclusively — reflexive in nature. This is expressed metaphorically in the idea of the *Übermensch*, the quasi-mythical being announced by Zarathustra as humanity's highest goal. This much-discussed notion is properly regarded as a metaphor for human integration rather than as any actual (or even potential) being of superhuman constitution of which the human species is a mere precursor, as the literal reading suggests. The *Übermensch* is no monster of superhuman dimension but a metaphorical expression of self-overcoming and self-creation, along with the other virtues practiced by the noble individual. The *Übermensch* is a key element of the countermyth Nietzsche proffers to unseat the Judeo-Christian myth he so despised.

In the suggestive notions of the *Übermensch*, the eternal recurrence, *amor fati*, and the will to power, Nietzsche attempts to put theory into practice, having maintained that a higher nature does not subjugate the affects but creatively transforms them through sublimation. Nietzsche's countermyth, in which each of these notions plays a part, is sublimated religiosity, a self-consciously metaphorical presentation of ethical and existential ideals expressive of exuberance rather than the decadence he perceived all around him. The *Übermensch* has "given style" to its character, abandoned "God" and dogmatic metaphysics, advanced "beyond good and evil," and overcome the "last man" within. It experiences *amor fati* and greets the prospect of eternal recurrence as a liberation. Eternal recurrence is not the cosmological, quasi-scientific doctrine for which it has often been mistaken and which the literal reading suggests, but is a test of the order of rank of its audience. The tentative "scientific" argumentation Nietzsche experiments with in support of eternal recurrence as a cosmological doctrine is such evident sophistry that it is remarkable such arguments have been taken seriously by some interpreters as indicative of Nietzsche's actual belief rather than the experiments and ruses that they are. The most important text dealing with the eternal recurrence remains the aphorism from *The Gay Science* in which the idea first appears, the "what if" clause of the opening sentence unmistakeably significant: "What, if some day or night a demon were to steal after you into your loneliest loneliness and say to you: 'This life as you now live it and have lived it, you will have to live once more and innumerable times more. . . .' If this thought gained possession of you, it would change you as you are or perhaps crush you. The question in each and every thing, 'Do you desire this once more and innumerable times more?' would lie upon your actions as the greatest weight. Or how well disposed would you have to become to yourself and to life *to crave nothing more fervently* than this ultimate eternal confirmation and seal?" (341) Nietzsche presents the eternal recurrence as a test of *amor fati* and rank, hence as an ethical and existential matter. Viewed in light of Nietzsche's philosophy as a whole, the eternal recurrence is not an independent hypothesis concerning the nature of existence but a metaphorical articulation of human existence in its highest form.

As a thinker and stylist, Nietzsche is frequently given to indirect, metaphorical, and quasi-mythical forms of expression, the non- or underappreciation of which has prompted many to mistake several of Nietzsche's most celebrated ideas as scientific or metaphysical postulates when their true connotations are of strictly human significance. Nietzsche is exceedingly fond of "what if" and "perhaps" statements as thought experiments designed to provoke and, frequently, to undermine received philosophical conceptions, often replacing them with less moribund and more interpretable ideas. Nowhere is this more true than in the notions of eternal recurrence and the *Übermensch*, ideas that if not understood metaphorically are at best silly and at worst dangerous. As allegories, on the other hand, they are highly suggestive possibilities of human integration, and it is here that their true value resides.

So conceived, the *Übermensch* conducts itself in accordance with the will to power in its highest manifestations, conforming to the will itself rather than to moral standards imposed from without. It recognizes rights only among its own kind, and then as a courtesy only. Indeed it is through an expression of generosity and personal egoism that the powerful type deigns to recognize anyone's rights at all or any other form of constraint on its will. In refusing harm to those of its kind, it is honoring itself more than others, the true object of respect being the aspect of oneself that one perceives in the other. Nietzsche suggests, "Perhaps it admits under certain circumstances that at first make it hesitate that there are some who have rights equal to its own; as soon as this matter of rank is settled it moves among these equals with their equal privileges, showing the same sureness of modesty and delicate reverence that characterize its relations with itself — in accordance with an innate heavenly mechanism understood by all stars. It is merely another aspect of its egoism, this refinement and self-limitation in its relations with its equals — it honors *itself* in them and in the rights it cedes to them."[6] The powerful individual cedes the rights it first claims for itself to others on the condition of equal rank, and then not as a requirement of impartial justice but as so much good manners, a case of *noblesse oblige*. "[A]s soon as this principle is extended," Nietzsche writes, "and possibly even accepted as the *fundamental*

principle of society, it immediately proves to be what it really is —
a will to the *denial* of life, a principle of disintegration and decay"
(259). Nietzsche repeatedly insists that "one has duties only to one's
peers; that against beings of a lower rank, against everything alien,
one may behave as one pleases or 'as the heart desires,' and in any
case 'beyond good and evil'" (260).

Here the contrast with decadence moralities is abundantly clear.
Whereas the morality of the powerful originates with an affirmation,
an exuberant yes-saying to its own form of life, one that only as a
secondary consideration generates recognition of others or others's
rights, slave morality originates with a recognition (of sorts) of
otherness. Specifically, it is the otherness of the highest type that
gains its attention. It is, moreover, a perception not only of an alien
nature but of a profoundly threatening one. Slave morality is premised upon negation in a fashion antithetical to master morality.
Its original evaluation is a condemnation of an enemy more powerful than itself and thus a threat to it. "The enemy" is its first cat-
egorization and creative act prior to any self-understanding or
self-affirmation, a representation containing a critical and neurotic edge wholly absent from epithets of the noble morality which
describe those of an alien nature — "bad," "ignoble," "base."
Whereas the latter epithets are expressive of contemptuous indifference toward inferiors, the slave's concept of "evil" betrays
fear of an altogether stronger and superior nature.

Physio-psychologically speaking, slave morality is a negation
and rebellion on the part of the ill-constituted against the well-
constituted, and ultimately against life itself. It is fundamentally a
gesture of negation in contrast to the exuberant self-affirmation of
the powerful, a mode of evaluation expressive of pessimistic suspicion, profound dissatisfaction with its condition and with human
existence in its entirety, a disposition to negate and condemn the
well being of higher natures, a keen sense of suffering, and a will
both to ease its condition and to undo the happiness of more powerful natures. Like all moralities, slave morality is "the symptom

of a certain kind of life."[7] What underlies it is the will to power of the resentful at the lowest rung of Nietzsche's hierarchy of human types.

As an expression of the will to power, slave morality constitutes an attempt on the part of the weakest to impose values expressive of their nature on all persons, most especially the powerful. Its element of creativity consists in unseating by inverting the values of nobility, replacing its virtues with those apt to ease the condition of the weak. This "slave rebellion" in morality is essentially a strategy to gain advantage over higher types by enlisting the latter into the cause of ameliorating the plight of the ignoble and elevating them into a hegemonic position. The strategy consists in poisoning the conscience of the noble by means of a religious and nihilistic worldview atop which stands not well-constituted humanity but a vengeful deity which holds a special place in its heart for the downtrodden of the earth. Beginning with Judaism and Christianity, aristocratic virtues are supplanted with a new set of values that equates virtue with suffering, servility, poverty, and physiological inhibition. This new morality declares: "'[T]he wretched alone are the good; the poor, impotent, lowly alone are the good; the suffering, deprived, sick, ugly alone are pious, alone are blessed by God, blessedness is for them alone — and you, the powerful and noble, are on the contrary the evil, the cruel, the lustful, the insatiable, the godless to all eternity; and you shall be in all eternity the unblessed, accursed, and damned!'"[8]

This victorious rebellion had its inception in the formation of a herd of ill-constituted natures. Collective formation eases the burden of existence in part by eliminating differences, strengthening ties of dependence, and abolishing the virtues of nobility. The weak, Nietzsche maintains, instinctively seek collective organization as a strategy in self-preservation, the individual being incapable of asserting its will to power independently, and needing the strength and security that numbers bring. Unable to stand alone, the weak form a herd of like souls divested of autonomy and dedicated to collectivized self-assertion. The values they prize are similarly collectivist in nature. Compassion, pity, modesty, and altruism are each symptomatic of human life in decline and betray a profound physio-psychological enervation. They express a nature incapable and resentful of higher achievement, exuberance, and wealth, one ill at ease with existence and inclined to seek nothing so much as ease and a respite from its condition. In a profound act of presumption, and with a complete lack of historical consciousness, the herd organization deems "natural" and unconditional its moral values, forgetting that its particular values were invented as strategic measures deployed in the struggle for hegemony. The values of the collectivity take on an unconditional and ahistorical character, their status as interpretations disappearing altogether from collective memory. "The good," in point of fact the will to power of the weakest, is equated with selflessness and declared to inhabit an otherworldly realm of absolute values, while "evil" — the original generative concept of slave morality — is substantively identical with the "good" of the highest type.

Ressentiment: *A Political Psychology*

For all the objections to which Nietzsche's philosophy of power and morality are vulnerable — a few of which I shall pursue later in this chapter — my principal interest here lies with the elements of Nietzsche's view that a contemporary philosophy of power must take seriously. It is an exercise in selective retrieval that I here undertake, on the conviction that the doctrine of the will to power provides a perspective indispensable to the analysis of power as it functions at both a political and social level.

Of abiding value in Nietzsche's depiction of social reality is the pervasiveness of the will to power, the operation of which he detects in patterns of action and intellection not typically associated with power seeking in its grosser forms. It is less the blatant forms of political power seeking that arouse Nietzsche's suspicion than those subtler forms that, precisely for reason of their subtlety and concealment, have been able to mask their operations. The power wielded by political tyrants, church, and aristocracy, which by Nietzsche's time had long since been clearly discerned, occupy him less than the more subterranean manifestations of power which arouse little suspicion for reasons of both their invisibility and their success. It is the will to power of the weakest that Nietzsche insists — in stark contrast to liberal and socialist critiques — has succeeded altogether in imposing its will on the strongest. The principal danger for human freedom lies not in the will to power of strong individuals but in that of the herd organization that European society had become. The reality of modern life is that civil society has become a mass society in which the ties of collective obligation and conformity pose a formidable threat to the values of individuality that Nietzsche prizes. A pervasive spirit of indolence has largely supplanted individual independence, leading us into ever more and ever larger collective groupings, the general mandate of which is to make life more secure and, invariably, more dependent.

What has prompted this widespread instinct for collectivization is *ressentiment*. Nietzsche employs the French *"ressentiment"* for reasons of its pronounced and persisting vindictiveness absent from its German and English counterparts. *Ressentiment* connotes ill-disposedness not only toward the ostensible object of its disaffection, but more subtly and more tellingly toward the general condition of its existence. The rancorous note with which it asserts its will or advances its demands is not adequately explained psychologically (or physio-psychologically) with reference to the particular object of critique and the injustice it has purportedly committed at the hands of the resentful individual, but betrays an underlying (one might say ontological) condition of being-in-the-world. This is the state of being of the ill-constituted, a condition the marks of which are incapacity, frustrated longing, and mediocrity, each symptomatic of life lived in a hostile environment.

Because of its incapacity, its mode of action is essentially reactive and conformist rather than spontaneous and *sui generis*. It would sooner negate than affirm, follow than lead, and tear down than create. Its psychology is premised on negation. It is a psychology that would sooner direct its gaze outward toward a demonized enemy than inward toward its unbearable depths. It requires the presence of an "Evil One," real or imagined, onto which it may transfer its ill will. It seeks the company of like souls on the condition that the collectivity adopt a moral stance at once consoling and hostile to an adversary. It willingly surrenders its freedom to the mass which in turn rewards it in the form of consolation and revenge. It is a psychology in which identity is contingent upon its antithesis rather than arising spontaneously from its inner depths. Its identity and conception of the good are articulated in express opposition to the form of life of the powerful (or those perceived as such).

To carry out its mandate, the collectivity requires the services of the "ascetic priest" or his secular counterpart. This individual *"alters the direction of ressentiment."*[9] Wishing to deaden the effects of its suffering, the resentful type directs its gaze outward to discover the cause of its condition, a scapegoat on which to vent its affects. The ascetic priest offers a new cause of its displeasure — its own sinfulness — and counsels new means of redemption. These include, in addition to the longing for an unearthly paradise: "the general muting of the feeling of life, mechanical activity, the petty pleasure, above all 'love of one's neighbor,' herd organization, the awakening of the communal feeling of power through which the individual's feeling of discontent with himself is drowned in his pleasure in the prosperity of the community" (III 19). Each of these measures constitutes a means of anaesthetizing the affects, not sublimating these to a higher end but deadening their effects on the suffering.

Through the repression of drives, collective existence is rendered tolerable. Yet in being turned back upon the self, the instincts of "hostility, cruelty, joy in persecuting, in attacking, in change, in destruction"[10] effect the origin of the "bad conscience." The collective struggle against displeasure in time brings about a condition of insipid domestication and normalization, described in a passage from *On the Genealogy of Morals*:

> The man who, from lack of external enemies and resistances and forcibly confined to the oppressive narrowness and punctiliousness of custom, impatiently lacerated, persecuted, gnawed at, assaulted, and maltreated himself; this animal that rubbed itself raw against the bars of its cage as one tried to 'tame' it; this deprived creature, racked with homesickness for the wild, who had to turn himself into an adventure, a torture chamber, an uncertain and dangerous wilderness — this fool, this yearning and desperate prisoner became the inventor of the 'bad conscience.' But thus began the gravest and uncanniest illness, from which humanity has not yet recovered, man's suffering *of man, of himself* — the result of a forcible sundering from his animal past, as it were a leap and plunge into new surroundings and conditions of existence, a declaration of war against the old instincts upon which his strength, joy, and terribleness had rested hitherto (II 16).

As a strategy in collective survival and a respite from its condition, the resentful, unable to give spontaneous expression to their drives, instead repress and internalize them. Their product is the "bad conscience" and the state of self-alienation described in the cited passage. The individual is progressively estranged from the instincts, rendered a function of the herd, domesticated, normalized, and alienated. No longer capable of significant individuation, the resentful settle into a condition of social conformity and normalized dependence. Any element of recalcitrant individuality that remains is perceived as a threat to their being and is anxiously held in check by the will to power of the mass.

Overlooking its fanciful and immodest presentation, Nietzsche's depiction of the moral-political psychology of *ressentiment* is of substantial value. For the number of times Nietzsche outrages us with his rhetoric and advances criticism that misses its target, still more often does it reach its target and reveal something hitherto unperceived. That it is the will to power less of the "rich and powerful" than of the mass of humanity — the will to power that conceals its nature behind a veil of moral catchwords — that ought to arouse our suspicion is an observation of lasting importance and that, at the very least, warrants the same attention that critiques from the left, asserting the antithesis, have long received. Marxist, socialist, feminist, postmodern, and liberal critiques of power most often overlook, or even fervently support, this will to power of the mass, content to countenance all but its most brutal manifestations. Indeed, the legacy of most of these critiques has been in the main to redeem ostensibly "emancipatory" movements of the left, as if emancipation rather than power were their true object.

It requires no extraordinary powers of discernment to perceive that it is not "liberation" — if by this term we intend human rights in the form of legal guarantees against harm — but power (in Nietzsche's sense) that is the ultimate end of such movements and of the mass of persons in "civil" society. Nietzsche's critique brings to light a political psychology well visible in his time and still more in our own. This is the psychology that aims to level social reality by reducing those whom it deems powerful to a condition of tractability and compliance. The rhetoric of "emancipation" often belies a psychology of *ressentiment* whose interest in liberation or equality is surpassed by an appetite for special advantages. Purportedly its rightful due in view of what it has suffered, its erstwhile oppressor must now accept an ostensibly equal and de facto subordinate position in the social order.

Nietzsche teaches the art of unmasking the politics of *ressentiment* and more generally of interpreting values as expressions of a will to power given to disguising itself behind a veil of evaluative epithets. Principles not infrequently are falsifications of the instinct for power. While Christian morality is the paradigm case, slave morality is not without contemporary and secular counterparts, and it is here that the will to power conceals itself with the greatest effect. Nietzsche's frequent references to socialism indicate that it is with this movement that he finds the politics of *ressentiment* most clearly manifest. Here the power instinct of the mass operates on the pretense of social justice and, prompted by a psychology of envy, asserts its will and takes its revenge. As Nietzsche writes in *Human, All Too Human*:

> Socialism is the visionary younger brother of an almost decrepit despotism, whose heir it wants to be. Thus its efforts are reactionary in the deepest sense. For it desires a wealth of executive power, as only despotism had it; indeed, it outdoes everything in the past by striving for the downright destruction of the individual, which it sees as an unjustified luxury of nature, and which it intends to improve into an expedient *organ of the community*. Socialism crops up in the vicinity of all excessive displays of power because of its relation to it, like the typical old socialist Plato, at the court of the Sicilian tyrant; it desires (and in certain circumstances, furthers) the Caesarean power state of this century, because, as we said, it would like to be its heir. . . . [I]t can only hope to exist here and there for short periods of time by means of the most extreme terrorism. Therefore, it secretly prepares for reigns of terror, and drives the word 'justice' like a nail into the heads of the semieducated masses, to rob them completely of their reason. (473)

Socialism is the means by which one class accedes to a position of hegemony, a political strategy invoked to attain neither justice nor emancipation but power. The politics of the left displays in full vigor the commiseration of the disaffected, the instinct for collectivization, the vilification of an adversary, the refrain of victimization, the presence of the ascetic priest, the demand for power redistribution, and the promise of an afterlife (the classless state, the Great Society). It knows best how to say no, to protest the agency deemed responsible for its condition, while affirming an uninspired brand of altruism.

While Nietzsche's remarks on the state do not form an altogether coherent conception of politics, and while many of these remarks are more of the order of provocations than sustained critique, their general tenor indicates an abiding concern for the fate of the individual in modern societies. Far from having nothing informative to say about politics, Nietzsche's critique of the state and of political moralities that sustain it is of lasting importance. It is a critique that incisively challenges the politics of the left and the critique of power associated with it.[11] Marxist depictions of liberal institutions as ministering to the higher strata while oppressing the lower is powerfully challenged by Nietzsche's critique, which asserts that it is precisely the latter that has gained the largest share of utility from these institutions. The most notable effect of liberal institutions, Nietzsche remarks, has been to normalize, domesticate, and level the condition of human beings for the benefit of the mass. To the detriment of human excellence and the freedom of spirit that is its principal condition, the modern state brings about a *"reduction to the herd animal,"*[12] the sacrifice of individuality to the leveling instinct of the mass. A phenomenon discernible in Nietzsche's time and more so in our own, the politics of the left habitually points an accusatory finger at the upper classes for allegedly identifying their interest with the common good while practicing a variation on the same theme. The outcome of this is a deterioration of the public sphere into a perpetual contest of competing wills to power, each engaging a war of rhetoric to the victors of which goes the title of guardian of the public interest.

Perspectivism and Critique

As noted at the outset of this chapter, Nietzsche views the will to power as a doctrine of extremely broad scope by no means limited to the sphere of politics. It applies to ethical relations, art, knowledge, and the individual's relationship with himself or herself no less than the political domain where its operations are most readily discernible. Its ubiquity in human life effectively removes the possibility of subordinating the instinct for power to the desire for justice or civility, as evidenced by manifestations of the will to justice that thinly veil a deeper motivation. The categories of political morality are ruses to be seen through and exposed by means of genealogical criticism rather than derivations of practical reason to be inspected for their logical credentials.

The method of critique that Nietzsche practices in his writings on morality and power must be understood in light of his opposition to the foundationalist and universalist premises of modern ethics and politics. The idea of philosophical reflection uncovering a foundation for evaluative statements or a rational decision procedure for resolving differences Nietzsche dismisses as an irredeemably ahistorical mode of thought which fails altogether to comprehend the essential perspectivity of reflection. Nietzsche rejects the myth of an Archimedean point, rational foundations, or a moral world order as bad metaphysics and untenable epistemology. In its place Nietzsche offers no universalist conception of right or the good but, as we have seen, a conception of values as expressions of an underlying physio-psychological constitution. In advancing criticism, he looks to neither the intentions nor consequences of moral action but to its origins in a given type of existence. Universal and impartial principles — guises of the will to power — give way to categories of "noble" and "base," "ascending" and "descending" life, categories that constitute critical perspectives for social phenomena.

Despite his unreserved contempt for all expressions of descending life, Nietzsche stands emphatically opposed to the universalizing pretension of all values, including those of the most powerful type. There is no unified set of values or form of life prescribable to all individuals and human types. Instead, there are numerous conceptions of the good that each have their proper domain and limits, both of which are determined by their respective points of origin — master morality prevailing among the powerful, and slave morality among the powerless. What Nietzsche condemns as a critic of morality is less the values of descending life than the tendency toward their universalization and absolutization, a tendency that has the effect of imposing slave morality upon higher types whose existence is properly governed only by their individual will to power. In a note contained in *The Will to Power* Nietzsche writes:

> My philosophy aims at an ordering of rank: not at an individualistic morality. The ideas of the herd should rule in the herd — but not reach out beyond it: the leaders of the herd require a fundamentally different valuation for their own actions, as do the independent, or the 'beasts of prey,' etc. (287)

The same idea occurs in *Beyond Good and Evil*:

> Moralities must be forced to bow first of all before the *order of rank*; their presumption must be brought home to their conscience — until they finally reach agreement that it is *immoral* to say: 'what is right for one is fair for the other.' (221)

Although Nietzsche is a strident defender of the values of individuality, he does not counsel an individualist ethic to all persons but only to the particular human type which he identifies as ascending. Indeed, the very notion of individuality as an affirmation of difference is one that expressly forbids general and substantive articulation.

The perspectivist thesis Nietzsche defends in his writings on knowledge and interpretation directly opposes the premise of modern epistemology that it is possible to attain knowledge that is conditioned by no point of view. Knowledge in all its forms is inseparable from perspective — a perspective composed of interests and will to power no less than historically conditioned presuppositions. It is contingent on both the interpretive vantage point of the knower and the methodology employed in argumentation:

> Henceforth, my dear philosophers, let us be on guard against the dangerous old conceptual fiction that posited a 'pure, will-less, painless, timeless knowing subject'; let us guard against the snares of such contradictory concepts as 'pure reason', 'absolute spirituality', 'knowledge in itself': these always demand that we should think of an eye turned in no particular direction, in which the active

and interpreting forces, through which alone seeing becomes seeing *something*, are supposed to be lacking; these always demand of
the eye an absurdity and a nonsense. There is *only* a perspective
seeing, *only* a perspective 'knowing'; and the *more* affects we allow to speak about one thing, the *more* eyes, different eyes, we can
use to observe one thing, the more complete will our 'concept' of
this thing, our 'objectivity' be. But to eliminate the will altogether,
to suspend each and every affect, supposing we were capable of
this — what would that mean but to *castrate* the intellect?[13]

An additional consequence of the failure of Enlightenment epistemology is that moral evaluation cannot be understood as an
aperspectival, ahistorical, or objective mode of reflection, but only
as occurring from an assignable and finite perspective. "[A]ll evaluation," he writes, "is made from a definite perspective: that of
the preservation of the individual, a community, a race, a state, a
church, a faith, a culture."[14] Like interpretation, "valuation is always
from a perspective,"[15] one composed of affects, interests, and interpretations without neutral standards. For Nietzsche, evaluation
is a species of interpretation. Knowing is the interpretive act of
attributing meaning to phenomena — of imposing form upon the
formless — there being no facts independent of the knower to comprehend nor any aperspectival location from which to comprehend
phenomena. Evaluation as well is an interpretive act that is wed-
ded to perspective and without a unified set of values to constitute
an absolute or neutral measure. Nietzsche repeatedly asserts that
"there are no moral facts whatever";[16] additionally, "there are no
moral phenomena at all, but only a moral interpretation of phenomena."[17] Values are themselves interpretations of human existence, an exegesis of phenomena and their significance to the valuer
or interpreter. Moral criticism therefore cannot constitute an impartial or neutral view of social phenomena as modern ethical theorists
have supposed.

The practice of moral criticism, accordingly, must operate within
limits defined by its interpretive and perspectival nature. The

method of criticism that Nietzsche adopts is what he terms "genealogy," a mode of interpretive analysis that looks to the historical origins of phenomena in order to uncover their moral significance. Genealogy is historical analysis that uncovers the will to power where conventional moralists would least expect to find it — at the origin of moralities and metaphysical worldviews. It is a profoundly suspicious mode of interpretation that detects the interests operative behind all ostensible impartiality, the affectivity behind all seeming objectivity, and the will to power behind the will to justice. Nietzsche's genealogy debunks the apparent "naturalness" of values, exposing the intrigue that belongs to their historical origins, the long forgotten affects and agenda that gave rise to the moralities of the present. Nietzsche relentlessly unmasks the "given" character of values as not only a failure of historical consciousness but a consequence of the dogmatism whose interest is served by concealing the ignoble origins of morality. The moralities of altruism and strong mutualism are well served by forgetting their histories since by the standards of these moralities themselves their historical inceptions and workings are scandalously immoral. Ethical codes that speak of love and compassion are rooted in a psychology of *ressentiment* and founded on collective hostility, often of an ethnically or racially inspired kind. The "chosen" are those locked in perpetual conflict with the despised race, the infidel, the hated other. Because the past survives in the present, the decadence moralities have an investment in concealing their roots while the business of the genealogist is to bring them to light.

What genealogy is not is a nonpartisan, value-neutral method of historical investigation. Its interest in history is far from purely antiquarian but is straightforwardly critical in intent. Indeed, it is stridently polemical in its description of human history. Genealogical interpretation is intentionally provocative, overtly partisan, and untamed in its moral verve. It contains an explicitly ethical dimension absent from conventional historical scholarship and aims to understand the past not for its own sake but as a means of dissolving its hold upon the present. To this end, it inquires into the purposes served by an impartial morality, and the interests advanced by its universalist values.

While genealogy as Nietzsche practices it is a bold, even fanciful, mode of criticism, it is one that remains mindful both of its interpretive nature and of its limits. Nietzsche never loses sight of the perspectival and partial nature of the criticism that he practices, refusing the appeal to universal or impartial principles demanded by modern moral philosophy. There is, he repeatedly asserts, no such perspective as "the moral point of view," no moral world order capable of providing the sort of epistemological certainty and metaphysical comfort sought by theorists of several modern schools. The critic of power and of social phenomena in general must not lose sight of the partiality of critical thought, in both senses of that term. Moral criticism is partial in disclosing only the particular aspects of phenomena that come into view from a given perspective, a perspective that is itself constituted by power, or the will to power, as well as by other affects, interests, and interpretations. Criticism is also partial in the sense that it is a partisan, even polemical, enterprise — an unavoidable condition given the interestedness essential to perspectivity. The critic of power can no more retreat to a standpoint devoid of interests, values, and power itself than the theorist of knowledge can retreat to an absolute standpoint of any description.

Yet it is this very issue of perspective that raises serious questions about the compelling force of genealogical criticism and ultimately about its philosophical value as well. Nietzsche's own premises lead us to ask from what perspective he himself speaks in his genealogy of morals. The answer would appear to be that he speaks from the vantage point of ascending human life, given that it is the nature of evaluative utterance to be nothing but an expression of a certain kind of life — ascending or descending — and given Nietzsche's identification with the former. An unmistakeably critical, evaluative mode of discourse, genealogy is itself a manifestation of the will to power of the genealogist, a will to power antithetical to what it takes as its object of interpretation or critique. The force of such a critique will therefore depend entirely on the perspective of the audience, with no standards to which one may appeal. The practice of criticism becomes itself a contest of the will to power, an interminable conflict of assertion and counterassertion.

As long as evaluation is viewed as a mode of physio-psychological expression, the prospect of a critique of power that is both incisive and philosophically defensible is dim. Genealogical critique necessarily leaves us with an unending struggle of competing wills to power without any philosophical avenue of mediation. It leaves us in the very situation that Nietzsche unmasks within the sphere of ethical relations and political practice, and without the resources needed to pronounce a philosophical critique — that could potentially be found compelling by those of a perspective other than the genealogist's. In the main, genealogical criticism preaches to the converted while to those of a differing perspective it is able at most to demonstrate that their morality fails by its own standards, thus constituting a form of immanent critique. It is unable in light of Nietzsche's expressivist conception of evaluation to appeal to either ethical or political standards capable of adjudicating rationally the contest of the will to power.

Contemporary evidence supporting Nietzsche's depiction of politics is all too abundant. The several elements of this critique — the psychology of _ressentiment_, the herd instinct, the vilified enemy, the instinct for revenge, etc. — all have their contemporary counterparts and together form an incisive perspective on social ontology. Nietzsche's profound suspicion of the appeal to principle is eminently reasonable in view of the frequency with which such appeals prove upon inspection to be self-serving rationalizations and falsifications of the will to power, yet that principled utterance can never be anything but this — that in principle notions of justice, democracy, or the common good cannot but be strategies in deception — is a conclusion that no amount of genealogical interpretation could satisfactorily demonstrate. A philosophically supportable critique of power must offer an appeal to principle, yet Nietzsche adamantly refuses this appeal. His refusal, coupled with the expressivist conception of value that underlies it, undermines the critical intent of his philosophy of power by preventing Nietzsche from pronouncing a principled objection either to political authoritarianism (the particular difficulty that the notions of master morality and the will to power inevitably raise) or to any other form of coercion. In place of principled critique Nietzsche offers an unprincipled and ultimately undecidable genealogy together with a "positive" doctrine of eternal recurrence, *amor fati*, and the *Übermensch*, a philosophy that affords no compelling alternative to the nihilistic expressions of will to power that Nietzsche condemns, only a countermyth. It offers a useful allegory for self-creation, but not the resources needed for a philosophically compelling critique of power. While the idea of human integration may itself furnish a useful perspective for critique, it is not as a principle but only as an expression of the will to power.

In sum, while Nietzsche's astuteness in detecting the operations of the instinct for power is perhaps unrivaled, his philosophy of power is unable in the final analysis to generate a critique of its operations that is rationally defensible. An unequaled "physiologist" of morality and power, as a philosopher of power Nietzsche fails to put forth — is effectively prevented from putting forth by his expressivist conception of value — a philosophically compelling ethical or political critique.

Two

Power/Knowledge

*I*n view of the pervading Nietzschean influence on Michel Foucault's genealogical investigations into modern practices of power, an assessment not dissimilar to that of chapter one applies no less to Foucault's genealogies than to Nietzsche's. In several respects, Foucault's problematic of power takes up where Nietzsche leaves off, with a configuration of philosophical premises, moral-political concerns, and interpretive methods derived from Nietzsche's thought and applied in a series of inquiries into forms of power endemic to modern practices. Foucault proposes to unmask hitherto unperceived expressions of power from the standpoint of the situated critic or genealogist, a perspective that eschews theoretical knowledge in its several forms while retaining a critical intent.

Following Nietzsche, Foucault conceives of power less as the singular possession of a centralized agency such as the state than as a ubiquitous phenomenon (or phenomena) in social and discursive practices. Power is profoundly misconceived, Foucault maintains, as proceeding on a purely "top-down" basis rather than from the "bottom" up, as historical interpretation reveals. Power is an altogether dispersed, decentralized, ubiquitous, and ineluctable phenomenon, a notably dissimilar conception of power to that presupposed by the modern state, a principal function of which is to circumscribe the reach of power, to limit its operations, and as Foucault fancifully expresses it, to "speak the truth to power." The problem that Foucault's analysis of power/knowledge raises for the modern state is identical to that posed by Nietzsche's conception of the will to power: if the reach of power in fact extends far beyond what was ever conceived by the framers of modern political institutions, the prospect of a social order effectively reigning in power or anaesthetizing its effects appears an unlikely proposition. Could political institutions ever limit power thus conceived, given the frequency with which its operations raise serious questions of justice? Further, what method of critique is appropriate to the detection of the forms of power that preoccupy Foucault, and what method is possible given Foucault's philosophical frame of reference?

Foucault's efforts to fashion a critique of power may be understood in relation both to Nietzsche and, by contrast, to the Frankfurt School of social criticism, most especially as represented in the writings of Jürgen Habermas (the topic of chapter three). Foucault defines his project in part as an attempt to replace the ideal of theoretical systematicity characteristic of the critique of ideology with a more limited and modest view of social criticism. While as critical as the latter of several forms of power inherent to modern culture, Foucault is deeply suspicious of all attempts to fashion judgments from the perspective of reason, truth, or universal principles of morality. Foucault makes no attempt, furthermore, to conceive of the critique of power within Marxist categories of ideology and science, a dichotomy very much operative within Habermas's thought. Moral criticism, for Habermas, is a dimension of explanatory science that positions itself in opposition to false consciousness or ideology — the latter being conceived as communicative distortions that conceal from persons the truth of their condition. For Foucault, such a scientific hierarchy of discourses serves merely to conceal the perspectivity of knowledge and to lend false legitimacy to a single interpretive perspective, namely that of Marxist politics. Foucault abandons the search for a suprahistorical or totalizing standpoint for social criticism along with the project of theory construction which would legitimize the role of universal judge. Foucault abandons as well the ideal of power-neutral communication at the heart of Habermas's theory of critique. Foucault regards the ideals of power-free discourse and a power-free society as dangerously utopian, and proposes to replace ideology critique with specific historical investigations of the forms of power endemic in modern society.

The argument of this chapter is that while Foucault's genealogical investigations reveal much about modern practices of power, they contain methodological tensions that limit their critical force. In view of his substantial indebtedness to Nietzsche, it is no surprise that Foucault at times encounters much the same difficulties that beset Nietzsche's efforts to fashion a compelling critique of power. Foucault's genealogies and ethics provide limited philosophical resources with which to articulate such a critique, to distinguish just from unjust forms of power, or to propose a compelling alternative to the forms of power/knowledge he incisively detects. The argument that follows addresses the status of genealogy, the standpoint of the genealogist, and the limits of genealogical criticism.

The Ubiquity of Power

Without granting to power the status of an overarching explanatory principle, the workings of power are the principal focus of Foucault's historical or genealogical writings. These investigations take as their objects the multiple forms in which power is exercised within modern social and discursive practices. Unlike the ideology critics, Foucault does not confine his analysis to the effects of powerful interests or centralized authority. Power is misunderstood as the private possession of an agent, whether individual, state, church, or institutions. Such a representation overlooks the multiple ways in which power is exercised without a specific agent of domination. Without denying or minimizing the importance of state power, the principal objects of Foucault's critique are those exercises of power that are "capillary" and which in a sense make centralized domination possible. Genealogy traces the effects of strategies which, while decipherable, are frequently without malicious intent and are just as frequently authorless. It reveals how power is exercised not on a top-down basis but from the bottom up, how relations of inequality are circulated and pervade a great variety of practices and institutions, and how they constitute the social domain as a totality. In short, genealogy documents how power relations have been able to operate and the specificities of their interconnections.

Foucault expressly opposes the "juridical" conception of power associated with the liberal, socialist, and Marxist traditions. This conception, rooted in the contractarian tradition of Hobbes and his progeny, is oriented toward establishing the moral foundations of authority, and presupposes a view of power as "sovereignty," understood as the exclusive possession and dominion of particular persons or institutions. Sovereign power is acquired and possessed by identifiable agents, and includes the power of church and state, parents and censors, and other agents charged with the task of mediating conflicts with a view to the preservation of right. The embodiment of justice and the good, the sovereign stands at some remove from the persons whose conflicts it impartially adjudicates. Obedience is the payment elicited by the sovereign as recompense for the protection of civil order.

The juridical conception of power, Foucault argues, provides an inadequate analysis of modern practices of power, harking back as it does to the political power of premodern times represented by the figures of the king, the aristocracy, and the church. "At bottom," he writes, "despite the differences in epochs and objectives, the representation of power has remained under the spell of monarchy. In political thought and analysis, we still have not cut off the head of the king."[1] A conception of power adequate to modern practice must comprehend fully its decentered and dynamic

constitution as well as the multiplicity and ubiquity of its operations. Power is no reified entity which one could acquire and hold
in one's possession, but rather "is employed and exercised through
a net-like organization."[2] It is "deployed" throughout a network of
practices and institutions, impressing on the subject from all di-
rections and orienting both its cognitions and conduct. It comprises
a system of vast scale, is composed of mechanisms of varying descriptions and proportions, and is alternately menacing and benign.

Modern power structures accumulate knowledge of populations
and of individual subjects that is both intrusive and systematic.
They attain this within practices of documentation and surveillance,
including examinations — scholastic, medical, psychiatric, etc. —
and histories — employment, criminal, sexual — the concerted
function of which is to elicit and constrain behavior by increasing
its visibility. Initially means of identifying and containing specific
social dangers, in time these practices gained broader scope within
an order of scientific knowledge and utilitarian rationality. Their
operations assume the function of enhancing the well being and
productive capacity of the persons subjected to them. Techniques
of surveillance, often incorporated into the very architecture of institutions, ensure a condition of hypervisibility. Power in this form
is as anonymous as it is ubiquitous, distributed as it is throughout
a vast network of institutions, professions, and practices, each possessing its function within the larger order. Its outcome is the
"carceral" or "disciplinary society" of modern times.

The disciplinary society is famously represented in *Discipline
and Punish* in the metaphor of the Panopticon, a prison designed
by Jeremy Bentham "to induce in the inmate a state of conscious
and permanent visibility that assures the automatic functioning of
power."[3] By means of constant surveillance (or the possibility of
constant surveillance) by guards themselves invisible to the prisoner, the circular design of the Panopticon induces within the
inmate a discipline that is largely self-imposed. The principle
of discipline, Foucault observes, underlies modern institutions of

power from prisons to factories, barracks, workshops, hospitals, and schools, each of which renders the individual an agent of its incarceration. The subject is held fast within a "swarming of disciplinary mechanisms" (211), a net-like configuration of power set upon it from all sides. Essential to the disciplinary society are both hypervisibility and techniques of normalization made possible by the gathering of knowledge regarding population norms. The practice of "normalizing judgment" governs the scholastic, medical, psychiatric, sexual, and other aspects of human existence, and has the double effect of enjoining homogeneity while individuating the subject within a field of normality and deviance. "In a sense, the power of normalization imposes homogeneity; but it individualizes by making it possible to measure gaps, to determine levels, to fix specialities and to render the differences useful by fitting them one to another" (184). By scrupulously surveying, disciplining, or incarcerating the subject, techniques of normalization diminish possibilities of human freedom and bring about a general enervation of social life.

As incisive as Foucault's analysis of social and political power is, he is no less concerned with epistemic power, particularly within the human sciences. The concept of power/knowledge is central to much of Foucault's work, in particular within the genealogical writings. In direct contrast to the critics of ideology who, following in the Marxist tradition, assert that statements, to be constituted as knowledge, must be emancipated from all vestiges of domination, and who hold out the possibility of objective and rational adjudication, Foucault refuses to separate interested from neutral, subjective from objective, discourse. There is, Foucault holds, no knowledge outside of power relations, no neutral method of adjudicating competing truth-claims. Knowledge does not presuppose the suspension of power relations, but requires the latter as a condition of possibility. Nor are power and knowledge antithetical, such that truth could appear only once the effects of power that conceal the truth are suspended. Rather, knowledge and power are correlative. In addition to being an instrument of domination, power has a productive capacity in the constitution of knowledge. Foucault writes, "We must cease once and for all to describe the effects of power in negative terms: it 'excludes', it 'represses', it 'censors', it 'abstracts', it 'masks', it 'conceals'. In fact, power produces; it produces reality; it produces domains of objects and rituals of truth."[4] Without collapsing the distinction between power and knowledge altogether, Foucault maintains that the two "directly imply one another; that there is no power relation without the correlative constitution of a field of knowledge, nor any knowledge that does not presuppose and constitute at the same time power relations" (27). Accordingly, power resides less in ideological mystification than in the constitution of fields and objects of knowledge and in techniques of adjudication. It is visible in the establishment of regimes of truth and the suppression of statements not conforming to authoritative and ostensibly rational criteria of adjudication.

The genealogical writings document as well the political dimension of identity or the manner in which power reaches into and fashions the constitution of individuals. Not only social practices and institutions, but relations between individuals and public institutions, penitent and confessor, psychiatrist and patient, student and teacher, prisoner and penitentiary, contain expressly political dimensions. The fundamental manner in which persons are constituted as subjects is an essentially political phenomenon. Subjectivity is fashioned within a network of subjugations, from the imposition of behaviors to the manipulation of desire and the workings of a variety of social processes. The human body is said by Foucault to be an effect of power, something that is disciplined and modified by everything from economic practice to medical technologies. One of the tasks of genealogy, accordingly, is to comprehend the human subject as at once an agent and effect of power relations.

It is thus that Foucault identifies the failings of political analysis that aims to depose power in all its forms. Such a view mistakenly conceives power as a reified item possessed and localized within specific sectors, and an obstacle to knowledge and truth. It fails to recognize the ubiquity and ineluctability of power, in addition to its epistemic significance and productive capacity. Despite the emancipatory intent of ideology critique and other universalist perspectives, Foucault insists that all such theoretical standpoints are inadequate to the tasks of detecting and critiquing the effects of power. The critique of power must instead trace power's effects across a variety of domains and document its operations through time.

Critique as Genealogy

Critical reflection, in Foucault's words, is a matter of "historical investigation into the events that have led us to constitute ourselves and to recognize ourselves as subjects of what we are doing, thinking, saying."[5] Following Nietzsche, whose genealogy of morals attempts to trace the history of ethics in order to reveal the will to power operative within modern standards of evaluation, Foucault's method of critique is similarly historical, interpretive, and partisan while oriented more closely toward modern institutions and practices of power. Without appealing to the will to power doctrine or other explanatory principles of equal scope, Foucault's genealogical writings constitute a collection of researches into the history and development of concepts, practices, and institutions governing modern social interaction. These disparate researches are never combined by Foucault into any kind of systematic whole in terms of which social reality as a whole may be viewed. Rather, the aim of these texts (principally *Discipline and Punish* and *The History of Sexuality*) is to bring to light the various assumptions and evaluations that underlie present modes of practice. Genealogical research (sometimes termed "effective history") serves as a reminder of what has been forgotten in modern forms of practice and subjectivity.

Without laying foundations for social criticism, genealogical inquiry disturbs what was thought solid and reveals the contingency behind all apparent necessity. It dissolves the self-evident quality of received judgments and reminds us how these judgments and the epistemic field within which they are constituted are historical constructions. Genealogy historicizes everything from the most everyday perceptions and intuitions to the great questions and problems that philosophers have often taken to be perennial. By placing everything within the rise and fall of history, genealogical analysis denaturalizes all that which we imagine necessary or fixed. It is the nature of power, particularly in its ominous forms, to present itself as having no alternative or as belonging to an unassailable order; genealogy aims to dissolve the dogmatic consciousness essential to its operations.

Genealogy is distinguished from traditional forms of historical scholarship, first, in its selective attention to events of the past that initiated intolerable conditions of the present and, second, in its refusal to interpret events as forming a continuous line of development from a single point of origin to a culmination in the present or future. While genealogy investigates the origins of various phenomena, it searches for origins in myriad places, examining a multiplicity of factors that have given rise to present conditions. Foucault is critical of historical research that subordinates the particularity of events to overarching mechanisms and explanatory schemes. There are, in his view, no underlying laws or metaphysical necessities operative behind the particularities of historical development, no fixed patterns or final culminations in terms of which to structure the past. Foucault's concern is to preserve and "record the singularity of events outside of any monotonous finality,"[6] without invoking theories of progress or uninterrupted continuity in history. In recording the accidents and the errors that gave rise to modern practices, the complexity and contingency of historical events, genealogy undermines the reassuring predictability of traditional historical investigation.

Because Foucault, like Nietzsche, upholds a perspectivist view of knowledge in all its forms, including historical research, he is no more capable of occupying a suprahistorical vantage point than the historians whose methods and principles Foucault expressly rejects. There is no standpoint available from which to identify teleological movement in history or to gain a totalized understanding of the past, present, or future. Instead, this method requires detailed investigation into the constitution of modern forms of knowledge and the variety of ways in which subjectivity has been constituted. The genealogist identifies how modern forms of self-understanding emerge through conformity to often unreflective evaluations and practices.

Above all, genealogy opposes itself to universalist and quasi-scientific modes of historical analysis such as historical materialism. It claims neither the status of a science nor to "vindicate a lyrical right to ignorance or non-knowledge."[7] Foucault looks with suspicion upon Marxists and others who view their method of critique as bestowing definitive insight into human affairs. To the question of whether genealogy is or is not a science, Foucault writes:

> It is surely the following kinds of questions that would need to be posed: What types of knowledge do you want to disqualify in the very instant of your demand: 'Is it a science'? Which speaking, discoursing subjects — which subjects of experience and knowledge — do you then want to 'diminish' when you say: 'I who conduct this discourse am conducting a scientific discourse, and I am a scientist'? Which theoretical-political *avant-garde* do you want to enthrone in order to isolate it from all the discontinuous forms of knowledge that circulate about it? When I see you straining to establish the scientificity of Marxism I do not really think that you are demonstrating once and for all that Marxism has a rational structure and that therefore its propositions are the outcome of verifiable procedures; for me you are doing something altogether different, you are investing Marxist discourses and those who uphold them with the effects of a power which the West since Medieval times has attributed to science and has reserved for those engaged in scientific discourse (84–85).

The "tyranny of globalizing discourses" (83) Foucault rejects along with the scientific hierarchization of knowledges. Replacing these are local narratives and forms of criticism which do not depend on "established regimes of thought" (81).

Whereas traditional historical investigation typically searches for evidence of continuous development, deep structures, and hidden meanings, the genealogist accentuates historical discontinuity, the accidental character of events, and the superficiality of all ostensibly deep meanings. Historical developments represent particular strategies in the struggle for power, the succession of one form of domination after another. Behind interpretations of concepts and claims to rational objectivity are found intrigues, conflicts, and treacheries of various descriptions. Genealogy documents how objective discourses and subjective motivations emerge together, how practices and institutions embody forms of domination, and how sinister intentions underlie modern standards of evaluation.[8]

For Foucault, social criticism depends on neither explanatory systems nor universalist theories of any kind. Thinking in terms of totalities — universalist theories of explanation such as psychoanalysis or Marxism — may be useful in conducting specific researches. However, Foucault becomes suspicious when the aim of such theories is to fashion an ahistorical standpoint removed from local realms of practice. He is particularly critical of those theorists who, speaking in the name of the universal or truth or justice, claim to distinguish knowledge from power, or science from ideology. This is expressed in an important distinction drawn by Foucault between what he terms the "specific" and "universal" intellectual. The latter, with the aid of either a universalist normative theory, a philosophy of history, or scientific knowledge, issues judgments concerning local practice from a distanced perspective not available to ordinary speakers. The "scientific" social critic, Foucault writes, is the modern heir of "the Greek wise man, the Jewish prophet, the Roman legislator."[9] What all continue to overlook is the extent of their own participation in the practices and discourses that form the objects of their criticism, and how their own reflection is made possible by the very power relations they seek to unmask.

What is needed, Foucault believes, is a reexamination of the intellectual's role in informing social practice in light of the Nietzschean doctrine of perspectivism. The specific intellectual, who Foucault in his genealogical writings understands himself to be,[10] is a radically situated critic who analyzes the specificities of practices and power relations from the participant's standpoint. Criticism requires a firsthand involvement in local struggles of various kinds and a concrete awareness of the specific practices and institutions that call for appraisal. Specific intellectuals are activists whose knowledge of the contingencies and techniques of particular domains of social practice enables them to identify contradictions from the vantage point of the participant. They analyze complexities and devise strategies for practice without recourse to totalizing theories of any kind. As Foucault writes, addressing the question of the role of the intellectual in social and political practice, "The intellectual no longer has to play the role of an advisor. The project, tactics and goals to be adopted are a matter for those who do the fighting. What the intellectual can do is to provide instruments of analysis, and at present this is the historian's essential role. What's effectively needed is a ramified, penetrative perception of the present, one that makes it possible to locate lines of weakness, strong points, positions where the instances of power have secured and implanted themselves by a system of organization dating back over 150 years. In other words, a topological and geological survey of the battlefield — that is the intellectual's role. But as for saying, 'Here is what you must do!', certainly not."[11]

Genealogy is characterized by Foucault as a method of criticism that always invokes local and popular forms of knowledge. Eschewing the universal intellectual's explanatory systems and theories, the specific intellectual favors particularly those local knowledges which have been demoted to a relatively low position in the scientific hierarchy of knowledges. Foucault speaks of an *"insurrection of subjugated knowledges,"*[12] by which he intends a rehabilitation by the specific intellectual of local discourses dismissed by regimes of universal knowledge for their apparent lack of rigor: "a whole set of knowledges that have been disqualified as inadequate to their task or insufficiently elaborated: naive knowledges, located low down on the hierarchy, beneath the required level of cognition or scientificity" (82). The claims of the participant, the activist, the doctor, the patient, the inmate, are taken up by the genealogist together with other forms of popular and local knowledge. They are rehabilitated not on account of their superior rigor or consensus-generating capacity, but precisely for their capacity to interrupt consensus and destabilize established power/knowledge configurations. Incapable of fashioning consensus, these subjugated knowledges serve as instruments of critique since they disrupt the self-evident appearance of what passes for truth and remind us how our present modes of practice came to be and, accordingly, may be otherwise. Herein lies genealogy's claim to radicality: as an iconoclastic mode of historical critique, genealogy — without issuing normative prescriptions — serves to challenge and destabilize forms of practice that have been imposed upon and have constituted modern subjects.

The Status of Genealogy

Among the questions that must be addressed in coming to terms with Foucault's thought are those pertaining to the status of genealogy. A question of special relevance for our purposes here is whether genealogy is an interpretive, and therefore hermeneutic, mode of reflection. As we have seen, Foucault is careful in distinguishing genealogy from scientific discourse and from certain traditional forms of historical scholarship which construe events as subsumable under totalizing explanatory systems. What is less clear is whether genealogy falls under the rubric of hermeneutic discourse. In addressing this question, Hubert Dreyfus and Paul Rabinow reply in the negative. Their reasons for doing so, however, are worth noting. While these commentators point out that gene- alogy is an interpretive practice, they insist on separating it from hermeneutic interpretation. They argue that genealogical interpre- tation renounces the quest for fixed and determinate meanings be- hind social phenomena, admits that behind every meaning and every perspective lies another meaning and another perspective, and acknowledges that it will never gain a wholly detached per- spective upon human history. Dreyfus and Rabinow cite Foucault's remark that "[i]f interpretation is a neverending task, it is simply because there is nothing to interpret. There is nothing absolutely primary to interpret because, when all is said and done, underneath it all everything is already interpretation."[13] They point out that interpretation fails to uncover anything deeper or more intrinsic than other interpretations which have been imposed arbitrarily by previous speakers. "In this discovery of groundlessness the inher- ent arbitrariness of interpretation is revealed. For if there is noth- ing to interpret, then everything is open to interpretation; the only limits are those arbitrarily imposed" (107).

Dreyfus and Rabinow operate here with a notion of hermeneu- tics that harks back to the romantic hermeneutics of Friedrich August Wolf, Friedrich Schleiermacher, and Wilhelm Dilthey, ac- cording to which the aim of interpretation is to uncover the origi- nal meaning of a text, which is conceived as corresponding to authorial intention. Surprisingly, their conception even of what Paul Ricoeur has called the hermeneutics of suspicion presupposes a view of interpretation as a search for the final truth of the text. This is by now an odd reading of the term "hermeneutics," given the turn hermeneutics has taken since Gadamer toward acknowl- edging the perspectivity of interpretation and away from all talk of essentialist meaning. It is a particularly questionable reading of Ricoeur's hermeneutics of suspicion, a mode of interpretation that (as we shall see in chapter four) makes no appeal to objectively determinable meanings or final truths of any kind. In addition to sharing Heidegger's and Gadamer's skepticism regarding essentialist meaning, the hermeneutics of suspicion is given to much the same mode of demystification as that found in Nietzsche's and Foucault's writings. Indeed, Nietzsche's genealogy of morals — from which Foucault takes much of his inspiration — is identified by Ricoeur as a paradigm case of suspicious hermeneutics. The latter shares with genealogical interpretation, first, the view that consciousness is primarily false consciousness and, second, a penchant for unveiling what present modes of understanding conceal.[14] The only seeming difference between Foucaultian genealogy and hermeneutic reflection is that, for Foucault, acknowledging the interpretive nature of social criticism also forces us to grant its arbitrariness. The premise that interpretation must either constitute a revelation of essentialist meaning and final truth or remain a matter of arbitrary decision is one that later portions of this study will endeavor to refute.

A further question regarding the status of genealogy concerns the standpoint of the critic. In reading Foucault's texts, one wonders from what perspective he himself speaks as an historian and critic of the disciplinary society. Given his Nietzschean commitment to the perspectivity of interpretation and his opposition to the methods of the universal intellectual, it is obviously not the case that the genealogist occupies any kind of external or ahistorical vantage point unavailable to other speakers. Foucault indeed goes out of his way to insist that he does not speak from a position exterior to current forms of practice and power/knowledge. Yet as a critic of such practices and power relations, he does assume a distanced perspective in calling into question the apparent necessity of modern institutions, the perennial character of modern philosophical problems, and the various practices that he investigates. Distance seems a necessary condition for a critique that would loosen the hold of its object upon consciousness. Given that the forms of power/knowledge that the critical historian takes as objects of reflection have themselves constituted the interpreting subject, from where does Foucault speak in the genealogical writings? If it is not from the perspective of any universalist theory or principled standpoint, then from the standpoint of which local practices, discourses, or traditions?

Although Foucault does not address either question straightforwardly, it is difficult to resist the impression that in averting such questions he claims for himself a kind of quasi-neutrality of the kind that his premises expressly forbid. Charles Taylor, making the same observation, remarks, "And indeed in his major works, like *The Order of Things* and *Discipline and Punish*, Foucault *sounds* as though he believed that, as an historian, he could stand nowhere, identifying with none of the *epistemai* or structures of power whose coming and going he impartially surveys."[15] Foucault's refusal to systematize his various researches in the manner of the universal intellectual and his expressions of opposition to normative foundations and totalizing theories are the closest he comes to answering these questions. Yet such statements fail to resolve the matter, and give every appearance of avoiding the issue. They would suffice as replies only if we were compelled to choose between the following options: the critic of power must speak either from a neutral, objective, and systematic frame of reference or from a position that is at once nowhere and everywhere. One of the principal aims of the chapters that follow is to show how this dichotomy may be subverted.

To Foucault it is imperative to avoid falling back into foundationalist talk of grounding critical reflection in a privileged discourse. All talk of normative foundations, he maintains, merely constitutes another attempt to impose a particular power/knowledge configuration, to create a new hierarchy of knowledges, and in so doing to disqualify, marginalize, and subjugate numerous other modes of discourse. However, the very notion of critique seems to presuppose, as a condition of intelligibility, an affirmation of some particular set of values or principles. One always recounts from a particular standpoint as Foucault, following Nietzsche, readily acknowledges, thus assenting, tacitly or explicitly, to a horizon of understandings and evaluations. Every expression, including every statement of opposition, requires a tacit affirmation; every criticism and evaluation makes an implicit appeal to a good, something from the perspective of which the criticism is intelligible. Yet Foucault remains oddly silent not only about the standpoint of the genealogist but about the values affirmed from that standpoint.

Taylor has noted that the concept of power also requires certain correlative notions as conditions of intelligibility. A critique that takes power relations as its principal object must rest on an implicit appeal to freedom, since a critique of domination has force only given a prior commitment to removing unwarranted constraints and impositions on human action.[16] Since genealogy is an exercise in unmasking, it must also invoke the concept of truth. Taylor writes, "The truth here is subversive of power: it is on the side of the lifting of impositions, of what we have just called liberation. The Foucaultian notion of power not only requires for its sense the correlative notions of truth and liberation, but even the standard link between them, which makes truth the condition of liberation. To speak of power, and to want to deny a place to 'liberation' and 'truth,' as well as the link between them, is to speak incoherently."[17] There are passages in Foucault's writings where he appears to grant that the aim of genealogical critique is indeed emancipatory — specifically the emancipation of subjugated knowledges and the undermining of present power/knowledge configurations. In *Power/Knowledge*, for instance, he writes, "By comparison, then, and in contrast to the various projects which aim to inscribe knowledges in the hierarchical order of power associated with science, a genealogy should be seen as a kind of attempt to emancipate historical knowledges from that subjection, to render them, that is, capable of opposition and of struggle against the coercion of a theoretical, unitary, formal and scientific discourse" (85).

Similarly, in "The Subject and Power," he proposes that "the

political, ethical, social, philosophical problem of our days is not
to try to liberate the individual from the state, and from the state's
institutions, but to liberate us both from the state and from the type
of individualization which is linked to the state."[18] Such affirma-
tions are puzzling given Foucault's express opposition to normative standards and principles. He would certainly deny freedom
the status of a universal principle, yet both the force of his critiques and the intelligibility of the concept of power seem to presuppose this principle.

On one hand, Foucault wishes to bracket normative claims as
well as claims to truth. He refuses to integrate his various researches
into a unified perspective and precludes appealing to normative
principles of any kind. He insists that genealogy is a descriptive
enterprise that refrains from pronouncing judgments or recommendations concerning its object of investigation.[19] Yet, on the other
hand, genealogy is clearly a partisan endeavor which implicitly
valorizes not only freedom but also such political values as equality, difference, and respect. A specific moral horizon underlies Foucault's genealogical writings and gives them whatever force they
carry as social criticism. This tension is captured in Habermas's
fitting characterization of Foucault as a "cryptonormativist" whose
premises prevent him from accounting for the standards on which
his critiques implicitly rely.[20]

A reply one might offer on Foucault's behalf is that as a specific intellectual he speaks from the perspective of specific subjugated knowledges and the values that these comprise. As an activist,
his partisanship is fueled by commitments to various forms of local rebellion, such as those of "May '68." As a subject of the power/
knowledge configurations of modernity, he takes up the perspective
of one variant of the modern liberty/equality/fraternity triad. This
would represent genealogy as a mode of immanent criticism, a
method of undermining modernity from within its own frame of
reference.[21] Foucault certainly has it within his means to respond

along these lines. Yet such a response only raises further difficulties. Which variant of the liberty/equality/fraternity triad does
he defend, and for what reason? Which local rebellions and activist movements does he find compelling, and why? Which subjugated knowledges does he wish to emancipate, and why? Richard
Bernstein, placing particular emphasis on this last question, calls
to our attention the difficulty in Foucault of distinguishing those
subjugated knowledges that are worthy of emancipation from those
that are not: "For there are subjected knowledges of women, Blacks,
prisoners, gays, who have experienced the pain and suffering of
exclusion. But throughout the world there are also the subjected
knowledges of all sorts of fundamentalists, fanatics, terrorists, who
have their own sense of what are the unique or most important
dangers to be confronted. What is never quite clear in Foucault is
why anyone should favor certain local forms of resistance rather
than others. Nor is it clear why one would 'choose' one side or
the other in a localized resistance or revolt."[22] Why are the events
of May 1968 singled out as a point of departure rather than the
events of October 1917? What conditions make the local rebellion
of the Polish Solidarity movement more estimable than the revolution in Iran?

A philosopher of Foucault's activist leanings should not need
reminding that in political practice we require means of distinguishing just from unjust exercises of power, desirable from undesirable
forms of emancipation, tolerable from intolerable social institutions. To warn us, as Foucault does, that "everything is dangerous"[23] is of limited usefulness when what is needed are means of
distinguishing tolerable from intolerable dangers. Do the dangers
inherent to modern penal institutions outweigh those of premodern
forms of punishment? Do the dangers associated with modern discourses of sexuality exceed those of earlier periods? Without the
identification and justification of a particular normative standpoint,
such questions appear unanswerable.[24]

The Limits of Genealogy

It is here that genealogy as a practice of social criticism encounters its limits. As a political counterpart of sorts to negative theology, genealogical critique attains clarity in informing us only from which perspectives it does not speak — neither from the standpoint of science nor from atop any supposed hierarchy of knowledges — which power/knowledge configurations it does not defend, and which normative standards it does not invoke. Genealogy is neither hermeneutic nor explanatory, neither liberal nor Marxist, neither rationalist nor irrationalist, neither this nor that, neither here nor there. Always operating from behind a veil of secrecy, Foucault the genealogist offers only the most cryptic of gestures indicating the place from which he speaks, the direction he favors, and the reasons why. When not inspiring an activism without principles, when not counseling "new forms of subjectivity"[25] (which ones?) or the emancipation of subjugated knowledges (which ones?), Foucault is reticent when it comes to offering recommendations or alternatives to the power relations that he uncovers.

Statements abound in Foucault's writings in which he categorically refuses to propose alternatives to the dangers endemic to modernity. In *Remarks on Marx*, for instance, he writes, "for reasons that essentially pertain to my political choice, in the widest sense of the term, I absolutely will not play the part of one who prescribes solutions. I hold that the role of the intellectual today is not that of establishing laws or proposing solutions or prophesying, since by doing that one can only contribute to the functioning of a determinate situation of power that to my mind must be criticized" (157). In an interview of 1977, Foucault responds thus to the following questions:

> 'Do you want the revolution? Do you want anything more than the simple ethical duty to struggle here and now, at the side of one or another oppressed and miserable group, such as fools or prisoners?' I have no answer. But I believe that to engage in politics — aside

from just party-politics — is to try to know with the greatest possible honesty whether the revolution is desirable. It is in exploring this terrible mole-hill that politics runs the danger of caving in.[26]

Foucault's interest as a critical historian clearly lies in the domain of contradictions, dominations, and tensions of various descriptions, and decidedly not in the realm of resolutions and alternatives. As an iconoclastic thinker, his principal aim is to disturb and to provoke. It is to unseat established regimes of truth and to reveal the origin and extent of the dangers besetting modern practices. Foucault is without doubt remarkably astute in tracing the development of such practices, in describing them in such a way as to highlight and preserve their essential complexity, and in cautioning against facile solutions to the dangers associated with them. Herein lies the considerable value that genealogy can claim as a mode of critical thought. It serves an important iconoclastic function by reminding us of the historical contingency of and the dangers inherent to present forms of practice. It undermines the dogmatism that can infect our moral and political attitudes by reminding us that all could have been otherwise.

Yet herein also lie the limits of its value. If we wish social criticism to be rationally or philosophically compelling, it must do more than alert us to the dangers inherent to our practices and include a reconstructive or "positive" moment. There is no reason to believe that undermining current forms of power/knowledge will of itself bring into being a more just state of affairs. Even iconoclasm is parasitic upon affirmation, and both are possible only once the normative standpoint of the critic is identified. There is no criticism without advocacy, no identification of social evils without a correlative valorization of goods. As certain more pragmatically inclined thinkers have noted, critical reflection must do more than demystify and debunk existing practice.[27] It must be complemented by an affirmative, reconstructive moment. Social criticism that lacks a sense of direction on account of its refusal to indicate the place from which it speaks and the values that it affirms, is of limited usefulness. As a consequence of such reticence, we are left without means of making crucial distinctions and weighing competing dangers.

The turn of Foucault's later writings toward ethical concerns does little to rebut this line of criticism. While directly addressing the question of what kind of ethics it is possible to fashion after the collapse of foundationalism, Foucault's proposal is a return of sorts to Nietzschean aestheticism. Since we now understand the contingency underlying modern forms of subjectivity and no longer regard the self as a metaphysical given, we are free "to create ourselves as a work of art," "to 'give style' to one's character" as Nietzsche proposed in *The Gay Science*. As Foucault puts it, "What strikes me is the fact that in our society, art has become something which is related only to objects and not to individuals, or to life. That art is something which is specialized or which is done by experts who are artists. But couldn't everyone's life become a work of art? Why should the lamp or the house be an art object, but not our life?"[28] Ethics becomes transformed in Foucault's later writings into a question of the self's relationship with itself, of how one may fashion oneself as a subject of one's own actions. On this aesthetic model, ethics becomes a kind of "*rapport à soi.*"

One wonders what becomes of other persons within such a conception of ethics. What becomes of the values of freedom, equality, tolerance, and respect for difference central to the genealogical writings when the domain of ethics has been restricted to aesthetic self-creation? The political dimension that Foucault finds all-pervasive in human affairs, that effectively prevents us from separating the political from the scientific, the historical, and so on, is not mentioned in his conception of the ethical — one area where even one who is not in the least sympathetic to Foucault would expect to find a political dimension.

Foucault's reticence is a logical consequence of two factors. The first is his refusal to identify the standpoint from which genealogical critique proceeds. The quasi-neutrality with respect to evaluations and the refusal to propose alternative power/knowledge configurations is traceable to his insistence upon not occupying any normative standpoint, not standing within any tradition or horizon of interpretation. Unlike the original genealogist of morals, whose critique of slave morality and the politics of *ressentiment* is clearly situated within a perspective of "ascending life," and who is consistent in carrying over his perspectivism into his ethical thought, Foucault makes it seem as if he could stand nowhere at all. The second factor is Foucault's view of interpretation. If social criticism is an interpretive enterprise, and if interpretation is not only perspectival but decisionistic, the prospect of fashioning or advocating alternative social arrangements with some claim to reasonableness is dim indeed. This conception of interpretation leaves us with a capacity only for unreasoning protest and without any principled means of preventing the arbitrary succession of one will to power after another.

Identifying the limits of genealogical criticism does not suggest that Nietzsche's and Foucault's historical investigations fail in their aim of uncovering operations of power that escape our notice or are concealed behind received understandings. Indeed, the genealogical writings of both authors are consistently and often remarkably illuminating. Nor does it suggest that genealogy fails altogether as a method of social criticism. The Nietzschean/Foucaultian impulse is to provoke and unseat, to unravel perspectives from within their own frame of reference rather than to critique them from an external perspective. This is one of the methods available to social criticism, particularly to the style of interpretation known as the hermeneutics of suspicion. Often the critic's task is to deconstruct from within, a method that suffices in many cases to expose its object and to persuade its audience. The difficulties that I have identified emerge only when social criticism is all there is, rather than unmasking and provocation serving as a preliminary moment to an affirmation intelligible to those not already sharing our perspective. This is a critique I shall direct at a later stage to other schools of thought — including a common interpretation of hermeneutics — that limit criticism to a radically perspectivist or immanent (in the usual sense) variety. If the project of social criticism, as I shall argue in chapter four, comprises both suspicion and affirmation, it is within the former that genealogy finds its place and value. Yet it is a project that, to be brought to completion, requires a complement beyond genealogy that can account for its own standpoint and the values that comprise it. It is precisely in identifying this standpoint that the genealogical project itself, as well as criticism in its other varieties, gains its force.

THREE

The Critique of Ideology

*I*t would appear that the critique of power necessarily presupposes distance from power, just as criticism in general presupposes a vantage point at some (partial) remove from its object. Yet if there is no absolute standpoint for critical reflection — no Archimedean point removed from all contingency and all power relations — what sort of critical distance is possible? If social criticism is situated in a finite perspective which itself has a political dimension, how can power become an object of critique without generating an impossible circularity? Moreover, what sort of practice is social criticism, and what philosophical resources are available to it? These questions do not receive altogether satisfactory treatment in the genealogical conception of critique, which as it stands cannot escape the duplicity of insisting on the necessity of moral-political opposition while depriving the critic of any principled means of articulating such a critique. This concern is shared by Jürgen Habermas, whose philosophical project also receives much of its orientation from the questions that concern us here. Habermas, the leading heir of the Frankfurt School of social criticism, inherits those theorists' preoccupation with identifying a perspective from which to articulate a reasoned critique of social practices and institutions. In contrast to Foucault, Habermas takes much of his inspiration not from Nietzsche but from Kant and the Enlightenment project of providing a rational grounding for normative evaluation. Asserting that normative claims admit rational adjudication, Habermas argues that it remains the task of moral and political philosophy to provide a systematic grounding for social criticism, most especially for the critique of power.

Much of Habermas's project may be understood as an attempt to redeem the scientific credentials of the critique of ideology. Critical reflection is represented as a dimension of explanatory social science. Following in both the Kantian and Marxist traditions, Habermas undertakes a systematic project aimed at bringing together scientific investigation and normative evaluation. The overriding task of a critical theory of society is to provide an assessment of existing practices, institutions, and discourses from the standpoint of scientific knowledge. It is to make possible the emancipation of human beings from quasi-natural forms of domination and systems of ideology — primarily capitalist interests operative within liberal institutions — given an objectified grasp of society as a totality. In general terms, critical theory attempts to fashion a comprehensive explanation of social reality as a critical and scientific standpoint from which to counter the effects of false consciousness and enlighten its victims to the reality of their condition.

The argument of this chapter is that Habermas's critique of ideological power rests upon untenable assumptions regarding the practice of social criticism. The ideal of scientificity implicit to Habermas's critique is an ultimately dogmatic assumption which overlooks the essential perspectivity and partiality of reflection. In relying on unsupportable assumptions concerning its reflective status, critical theory fails to reconcile the need for a critique of existing practices with a recognition of the limits of human understanding.

The Science of Critique

While (ostensibly) cognizant of the situated character of normative evaluation and human reflection generally, Habermas's efforts are largely directed toward providing a justification for the perspective of objectivity, thus mitigating the claims of the radically situated (genealogical or hermeneutic) critic. Mindful of its own historical emergence, critical theory seeks to comprehend the process of historical development as a teleological advancement toward progressive emancipation. Critical reflection must at once adopt an objectivating attitude toward society while recognizing the conditionedness of its own discourse. Beginning from the premise that modern social and discursive practices are pervaded by power in the form of ideological distortions inhibiting self-understanding and concealing from persons the truth of their condition, critical theory assigns itself the task of exposing such mystifications. The practical intent of critical theory is to provide a scientific framework from which to critique existing practices independently of the workings of ideology and "hypostatized powers," a framework that will make social reform in the service of emancipation possible. Without advancing a particular conception of the good, this method of theorizing assists the process of emancipation by enlightening moral agents about the ways in which their practices and modes of communication inhibit autonomy. It discloses the various ways in which human fulfillment is threatened by sectarian interests and other forces of domination.

Critical theory represents a continuation of the Enlightenment project that would secure emancipation by means of a rational and foundationalist assessment of social practices. It seeks a theoretical grounding for social criticism and proposes to measure the course of human progress from the standpoint of scientific knowledge. At the same time, Habermas provides a critique of conditions he finds pervasive within modernity. Among these is the domination of a technocratic conception of rationality, one that assimilates issues of justice to problems of technical efficiency. The encroachment of the needs of systems (including the economy, the military, the bureaucracy, and so on) into the domain of politics has restricted the capacity for democratic discussion, while an instrumental rationality originally at home within the experimental and mathematical sciences also threatens to undermine the practice of egalitarian communication over matters of public concern. Following in the Frankfurt School tradition, Habermas views instrumental rationality as a potentially dehumanizing mode of thought as well as an obstacle to critical reflection.[1] The conception of rationality defended in Habermas's work is a communicative rationality, one that replaces the primacy of technical problem solving with an interest in open forms of communication.

While Habermas's critical theory is fundamentally oriented by the Frankfurt School tradition from which it emerges, it must also be viewed as an attempt to transcend the immanent criticism practiced by earlier members of this circle. It issues a challenge not only to the immanent criticism of Foucault but to that of Max Horkheimer and Theodor Adorno. For the latter authors (in keeping with Marx), the social critic does not occupy a vantage point external to the society being criticized. The role of the critic is to expose contradictions within the thought and practice of the existing social order. Critical thought for Horkheimer and Adorno is a juxtaposing of the professed ideals of a society with its actual practices, a demonstration of the ways in which the object of critique fails by the standards of its own culture. Social criticism in Habermas's view is a transcendence of the immanent. It is a reflective enterprise employing transcendental criteria and seeking a rational warrant for local institutions, norms, and practices. To Habermas, immanent conceptions of critique lack sufficient means of redeeming the principles on which they rely. These conceptions risk falling back into historical relativism since they cannot legitimate their own criteria of evaluation. When the norms of the society are themselves corrupted (and not only the practices and institutions with which they fail to cohere), a transcendental move is required in order for the social critic to acquire the perspective necessary to detect such corruption.

Habermas's theory of critique must be viewed as well in relation to philosophical hermeneutics, and understood as an attempt to incorporate certain of its premises (including the situatedness of reflection) while surpassing the latter in critical capacity. With Gadamer, Habermas defends the principle of communicative rationality and the practice of unconstrained dialogue in which it is animated. For both figures, communicative interaction is not only an aspiration of local political practice but is constitutive of humanity itself. While regarding interpretation as an important dimension of social investigation, Habermas believes that hermeneutical philosophy lacks the resources needed to fashion a critique of the practices and traditions to which, it tells us, we always already belong. Hermeneutics, Habermas asserts, subordinates the critical moment of social analysis to participation in the movement of historical tradition. Its openness to the claims of interlocutors in dialogue and its anticipation of truth in interpretation unduly limits the capacity of the social critic to speak in the role of objective observer. Its emphasis on participation within language and tradition also overlooks the extent to which language and tradition may harbor systematic distortions. As Habermas writes, "Language is *also* a medium of domination and social power. It serves to legitimate relationships of organized force. Insofar as the legitimations do not articulate the power relationship whose institutionalization they make possible, insofar as that relationship is merely manifested in the legitimations, language is *also* ideological. In that case it is not so much a matter of deceptions in language as of deception with language as such."[2] Hermeneutics, Habermas asserts, is incapable of detecting systematic distortions within forms of communication and interaction, and for this reason requires the supplementation of a critical theory of society. This theoretical knowledge enables the critic to surpass the competence level of ordinary speakers and import causal explanations of social phenomena. By introducing a neutral frame of reference from which to analyze social and discursive practices, the situatedness of the critic is mitigated.

The task that critical theory assigns itself, then, is to uncover the false consciousness inherent in tradition and language which preserves the legitimacy of the existing social order while concealing the various workings of ideology. Surpassing hermeneutic reflection, critical theory takes as its object not the "intersubjectively intended and symbolically transmitted meaning"[3] of interpretive understanding, but the "objective meaning" (187) of explanatory social science. It enlightens the victims of domination to the real meaning of the various components of the social system and to the reality of their predicament within that system. It reveals to these agents how their real interests have been subverted by the existing order: "The theory serves primarily to enlighten those to whom it is addressed about the position they occupy in an antagonistic social system and about the interests of which they must become conscious in this situation as being objectively theirs."[4]

Through a combination of hermeneutic and functionalist analysis, Habermas constructs a two-tiered theory of society as simultaneously lifeworld and system. Society may be comprehended both from the participatory standpoint of social actors and from the observational perspective of explanatory science. Social analysis thus represents a combination of hermeneutic interpretation of the significance of social phenomena with functionalist explanation of objective meaning — a combination of understanding and explanation. Thus, while such investigation is historically situated, it also incorporates a dimension of objectivity by viewing particular social phenomena as elements within a system. The power inherent to practices and institutions is seen as fulfilling certain functions within the social system, and it is in light of the contributions they make to the self-maintenance of that system that the meaning of such elements is grasped. Functionalism thus permits us to view tradition and language, as it were, externally — as empirically encountered components of the system of culture, their significance a function of their empirical connections and of the parts they play within a larger system. Since the connections between the various components of the social system are empirical in nature, the meaning of social practices and norms have the status of facts.

In this manner Habermas proposes to grasp the objective meaning of distorted communications, and thus transcend the perspectivity of hermeneutics and immanent criticism. Meaning may be grasped by explaining theoretically why certain values and beliefs came to be held: "The What, the semantic content of a systematically distorted manifestation, cannot be 'understood' if it is not possible at the same time to 'explain' the Why, the origin of the symptomatic scene with reference to the initial circumstances which led to the systematic distortion itself."[5] Critical social science returns to the origins of ideological mystification and explains its function within the social order. Critical thought surpasses hermeneutic reflection by investigating the factors operative behind the back of social agents — factors that, because repressed, "have the status of causes."[6]

Thus, at the heart of Habermas's theory of critique is an emancipatory knowledge made possible by self-reflection. Self-reflection reverses the repressive force of ideology by rendering conscious what ideology had concealed from consciousness. Once it is acknowledged that practices conceal unconscious and causal forces, self-reflection makes subjects aware of these conditions and dissolves whatever hold they have on consciousness. By showing how history embodies forced consensus and hidden power relations, self-reflection upsets the dogmatism of traditional practice. Theoretical insight is thus indispensable to the practice of removing barriers to emancipation and human fulfillment. Self-reflection also restores to individuals and social groups a true awareness of the position they occupy in a repressive social system. It constructs a systematic narrative documenting the formative processes of the human species from the point of view of the culmination of such processes, enabling us to view such agents as belonging to the movement of historical development.

While self-reflection, and the emancipation that it makes possible, is the aim of critical social science, its methodology is characterized by Habermas as "depth hermeneutical." Critical theory is modeled on the methodology of psychoanalysis, "the only tangible example of a science incorporating methodical self-reflection."[7] Habermas writes in *Knowledge and Human Interests*, "Psychoanalytic interpretation is concerned with those connections of symbols in which a subject deceives itself about itself. The *depth hermeneutics* that Freud contraposes to Dilthey's philological hermeneutics deals with texts indicating *self-deceptions of the author*. Beside the manifest content (and the associated indirect but intended communications), such texts document the latent content of a portion of the author's orientations that has become inaccessible to him and alienated from him and yet belongs to him nevertheless. Freud coins the phrase 'internal foreign territory' to capture the character of the alienation of something that is still the subject's very own" (218). Psychoanalytic depth hermeneutics surpasses what Thomas McCarthy calls "normal hermeneutics"[8] in taking for its object not only the conscious intentions of speakers but more importantly "the latent content of symbolic expressions, a content that is inaccessible to the author himself" (196). While psychoanalytic investigation may appear hermeneutic — as a dialogical interpretation of meaning between speakers oriented toward a common subject matter — and while Freud himself noted similarities between analysis and the practice of translation, the meanings that psychoanalysis uncovers occur not at the level of ordinary language but below the threshold of consciousness. A self-reflective science, psychoanalysis views behavior and linguistic expressions as manifestations of unconscious drives or as disguised expressions of repressed needs. They are explainable in terms of latent conflicts and causal connections between principles — as manifestations, for instance, of conflict between the pleasure and reality principles. Psychoanalytic procedures combine interpretation of meaning with explanation of causes, and it is only this combination that makes true insight into the subject's condition possible.

A further point of distinction between psychoanalysis and hermeneutic interpretation concerns the mode of communication between speakers in psychoanalysis. The psychoanalytic interview is not a dialogue in the hermeneutical sense of an interpretive inquiry between speakers in a symmetrical relation entertaining the claims of the other and acknowledging the possibility of their truth value. Unlike hermeneutic dialogue, which is a testing of interpretations and a risking of one's prejudices in an encounter with an interlocutor whose standpoint is different from one's own, and from whom one may have something to learn, the mode of interaction between analyst and analysand is one of clinical diagnosis and therapy. The psychoanalyst, in order to detect the deep meaning of the patient's utterances, must overlook their possible truth value and focus instead upon those expressions that betray conflict and reveal something about the original symptomatic scene. Since the analyst must endeavor to get behind linguistic expressions to the conditions of their genesis, the hermeneutical anticipation of truth is replaced with pedagogy. As Habermas puts it, "The disturbance of communication does not require an interpreter who mediates between partners of divergent languages but rather one who teaches one and the same subject to comprehend his own language. The analyst instructs the patient in reading his own texts, which he himself has mutilated and distorted, and in translating symbols from a mode of expression deformed as a private language into the mode of expression of public communication."[9] As an exercise in self-reflection, psychoanalytic practice is an enlightening and therapeutic discourse which aims at restoring the subject's autonomy.[10]

Habermas uses psychoanalysis to refashion the concept of ideology, transforming it from a conception dominated by economic categories to one rooted in language. Habermas characterizes ideology as a distorted form of communication, and thus an obstacle to consciousness in the same manner as psychoanalysis conceives of illusion and delusion. A form of false consciousness, ideology preserves the legitimacy of an existing power structure by concealing its capacity for oppression and by introducing substitute gratifications. The illusions it produces are rationalized compensations for repressed needs. By infiltrating ordinary language, ideological power conceals the contradictions of a social system, and in so doing ensures the continuing domination of certain groups within that system. Distorted communications stabilize oppressive practices and institutions by, for instance, concealing the ways in which they promote sectarian interests or by representing such interests as synonymous with the general will.[11]

The social critic plays a role in the domain of politics analogous to that of the analyst in the diagnosis of individual psychopathology. In both instances the analyst incorporates hermeneutic and explanatory procedures to uncover latent meanings and distortions within practices. Both serve a therapeutic and pedagogical function aimed at producing emancipation through the enlightenment of subjects under the spell of an illusion. Habermas realizes, of course, that this analogy is not without its limitations. In particular, the psychoanalytic conception of ideology as a form of communal neurosis faces a difficulty that Freud himself brought to our attention. Freud points out in *Civilization and its Discontents* that the diagnosis of illusions affecting whole communities cannot incorporate the same methods as those employed in the treatment of individual neurosis, stating that the "diagnosis of communal neuroses is faced with a special difficulty. In an individual neurosis we take as our starting point the contrast that distinguishes the patient from his environment, which is assumed to be 'normal.' For a group all of whose members are affected by one and the same disorder no such background could exist; it would have to be found elsewhere."[12] Since individual neuroses are understood as deviations from socially recognized norms, the diagnosis of such disturbances must presuppose that certain standards of normalcy — standards that allow the analyst to distinguish the normal from the pathological — are in place. Such criteria, however, are not scientific constructions. They are, Freud tells us, culturally relative. Since such norms are themselves under suspicion in cases of communal neurosis, the critic of ideology must employ methods different from those employed in psychoanalysis. The theory of neurosis that informs Freud's analyses of individual disturbances is also unavailable to the ideology critic. The latter must therefore introduce new theoretical perspectives.

Historical Materialism

In order for critical theory to gain scientific standing analogous to psychoanalysis, it must be able to document the historical development of the human species. It must gain a theoretical mastery of the notion of undistorted communication, and supplement this with a developmental account of the acquisition of communicative and interactive competences. In lieu of standards of normalcy, critical theory must overhaul its foundations by undertaking a reconstruction of historical materialism.[13]

The theory of historical materialism, then, is central to Habermas's critique of ideology. It differs from Marx's original formulation of this theory, first, by abandoning any link between a science of history and research in the natural sciences. Second, it avoids positing a macrosubject as the bearer of historical development. "Historical materialism," Habermas suggests, "does not need to assume a *species-subject* that undergoes evolution. The bearers of evolution are rather societies and the acting subjects integrated into them."[14] Third, Habermas refuses to view historical events as unfolding in a necessary, unilinear, and continuous manner; history provides no guarantee of unremitting progress and is subject to temporary regressions in the evolution of social processes. Fourth, learning processes are not limited to modes of economic production, but are operative as well in the dimensions of communication, conflict resolution, and — more important for our concerns — moral consciousness. Habermas preserves historical materialism's evolutionary explanation of social phenomena. The theory's original aims were at once explanatory and practical. In demonstrating how economic structures could be comprehended in terms of developmental processes, it provides a theoretical perspective from which to assess current economic practices. As an exercise in self-reflection, it also has a practical intent, namely emancipation from power relations through the science of critique.

More controversially, although dispensing with the more orthodox doctrine of the necessity, irreversibility, and continuity of historical development, Habermas also incorporates from Marxism a teleological conception of history. Through self-reflection, it is possible not only to identify the direction in which history unfolds, but to specify its telos as well. Social evolution is progressing toward a state of increasing complexity, and such evolution may be understood as a process in which subjects learn progressively to cope with such complexity. Learning processes occur in the domain of moral insight and communicative interaction, and not only in the sphere of production as Marx had supposed. Habermas explains that "the species learns not only in the dimension of technically useful knowledge decisive for the development of productive forces but also in the dimension of moral-practical consciousness decisive for structures of interaction. The rules of communicative action do develop in reaction to changes in the domain of instrumental and strategic action; but in doing so they follow *their own logic*."[15] The learning processes that constitute social evolution are thus conceived as the unfolding of a logic of individual and societal development reminiscent of Jean Piaget's developmental approach to cognitive psychology. Each discrete stage of maturation constitutes a higher order of complexity and is passed through in a specific order of succession.

Habermas's rehabilitated historical materialism traces the evolution of universal competences in several areas of social scientific inquiry. A unified account of ego development, the theory incorporates a collection of researches on universal competences in the related realms of interaction, language, and cognition. It brings together Habermas's work on universal pragmatics with Piaget's study of cognitive development, Noam Chomsky's theory of linguistic competence, and Lawrence Kohlberg's research on the development of moral reasoning. This provides an integrated theoretical framework with which to study the processes of maturation within individuals and societies, and the progressive elimination of barriers to human development. It seeks to demonstrate how history is unfolding in the direction not only of social complexity but of greater autonomy and mastery of moral and political discourse.

Of special importance in this project is Habermas's appropriation of Kohlberg's observations in the field of moral developmental psychology. Proposing that we view moral consciousness as a dimension of interactive competence, Habermas asserts that normative judgments may be explained from an evolutionary standpoint. Moral beliefs may be examined from the detached and scientific perspective of developmental psychology in the tradition of Piaget and Kohlberg. Kohlberg's research thus assists in furnishing a theoretical framework for social criticism.

As an evolutionary approach to moral consciousness, Kohlberg's theory posits an invariant sequence of stages in the acquisition of moral competence from preconventional through conventional to postconventional levels.[16] While moral agents progress through these stages at varying speeds, and while development may stop at any given stage, individuals can neither skip stages nor move from the higher to the lower except in cases of temporary regression. In addition to their invariant order of sequence, moral stages are characterized as structural wholes which solve problems in qualitatively different ways. Progression through these stages represents the normal course of moral development, and while such progression is dependent on corresponding cognitive development, Kohlberg maintains that it is the stimulation that comes with social interaction (particularly through opportunities for role-taking) that normally engenders moral stage progression. Kohlberg thus believes that he has discovered an "empirical foundation" (227) for the nineteenth century liberal faith in progress. There are, he claims, universal long-range trends toward the approximation of stage six reasoning which justify a faith in social progress and moral and social evolution. He writes, "The liberal faith is not a faith in the inevitability of progress by some iron law of social history or by some biological unfolding in the child. The liberal faith is, rather, that under conditions of open exposure to information and communication and of a degree of control by the individuals over their actions and the ensuing consequences, basic changes in both individuals and societies tend to be in a forward direction in a series of steps or stages moving toward greater justice in terms of equity or recognition of universal human rights" (233). This faith in the evolution of moral competence is supported, he maintains, by cross-cultural evidence of progression toward postconventional modes of reasoning absent from preliterate societies. Both individuals and societies undergo moral evolution, with each higher stage representing a closer approximation to stage six.

Kohlberg argues that a theory of moral development must do more than merely stipulate that what comes later in time must be in some manner superior to what precedes it. It must formulate criteria that demonstrate the greater philosophical adequacy of postconventional reasoning. Kohlberg proposes that the higher developmental stages exhibit superior cognitive organization and formal adequacy; each stage is characterized by greater differentiation and integration than the stages preceding it. The higher stages display greater differentiation between the moral "ought" and the assorted "oughts" of practical and instrumental reasoning. Moral values are similarly disentangled from other kinds of values; the moral value of the person, for instance, becomes increasingly differentiated from the person's instrumental value to society, status, and so on. The combination of greater differentiation and integration entails a more adequate state of cognitive equilibrium than that found at lower stages, as evidenced by empirical studies suggesting that moral agents always prefer higher to lower stages (when, that is, they are capable of understanding the mode of thought at a higher stage).

At work in Kohlberg's developmental account is a metaethical formalism which regards morality as a "unique, *sui generis* realm"[17] of discourse. The moral domain is independent of other realms of investigation, and normative claims are judged solely by moral criteria of rationality rather than criteria of efficiency or utility. Kohlberg does not claim value-neutrality for his developmental project, but situates it within the modern tradition of deontological and formalist ethics stemming from Kant. Having assumed a formalist account of moral rationality, Kohlberg writes that "the formal definition of morality only works when we recognize that there are developmental levels of moral judgment that increasingly approximate the philosopher's moral form. This recognition shows (1) that there are formal criteria that make judgments moral, and (2) that these are only fully met by the most mature stage of moral development, so that (3) our mature stages of judgment are more moral (in the formalist sense, more morally adequate) than less mature stages."[18] As well as better fulfilling formal criteria of moral adequacy, each progression in development is accompanied by a corresponding change in social perspective — from the "concrete individual perspective" at the preconventional level to the "member of society" perspective at conventional stages, and finally to the "prior to society" perspective at the level of postconventional, principled reasoning (177). The principles articulated from the prior to society perspective constitute those "standards on which a good or just society must be based" (178). It is only from this presocial standpoint that social practices and norms can be properly adjudged, and the principles generated from this standpoint are claimed by Kohlberg to be "intrinsically appealing to any rational agent; their appeal, unlike that of Stage 4 modes of reasoning, is independent of extrinsic social norms."[19]

Kohlberg and Habermas both argue that in order to characterize progression from lower to higher stages as a developmental or learning process, it is necessary to posit an end-state of moral development to serve as a reference point from which we could retrospectively describe such movement as learning (rather than merely a change in opinion). Both also agree that stage six universalism constitutes this point of reference, and that since it alone succeeds in fully meeting Kohlberg's criteria, stage six fully represents "the moral point of view." As Kohlberg puts it: "A formalistic normative theory says, 'Stage 6 is what it means to judge morally. If you want to play the moral game, if you want to make decisions which anyone could agree upon in resolving social conflicts, Stage 6 is it.'"[20] The moral rightness of any practice may be assessed by testing it against the judgment of those at the highest developmental stage. Kohlberg goes so far as to assert that, if his line of argument is correct, then "the only 'competent moral speakers' are the rare individuals at Stage 6 (or, more tolerantly, at Stages 6 and 5)" (182) — which, according to his figures, together total approximately 20 percent of the population of American adults (less than five percent of whom are at stage six).[21]

While seeking to avoid certain forms of what is sometimes called the naturalistic fallacy, this evolutionary account of moral reasoning, Kohlberg admits, does commit one form of this fallacy — namely that form according to which "any conception of what moral judgment ought to be must rest on an adequate conception of what it is."[22] A philosophically adequate moral theory must, as he puts it, "'work' empirically" (178); that is, the evaluations it prescribes must not fail to cohere with the judgments of those individuals who have attained the highest level of moral competence. Empirical propositions, while not proving the legitimacy of normative claims, nonetheless act as a test for such claims, frequently serving to falsify the latter. This makes for a view of the relation between philosophy and science (or moral theory and moral psychology) as one of mutual reinforcement. Habermas and Kohlberg both speak of a complementary relationship between normative and empirical statements. Discussing Kohlberg, Habermas writes, "The success of an empirical theory, which can only be true or false, may serve as a safeguard of the normative validity of a moral theory used for empirical purposes. . . . It is in this sense that rational reconstructions can be checked or tested, where 'test' means to investigate whether different pieces of theory are complementary and fit into the same pattern. Kohlberg's clearest formulation of this reads as follows: 'Science, then, can test whether a philosopher's conception of morality phenomenologically fits the psychological facts. Science cannot go on to justify that conception of morality as what morality ought to be.'"[23] Kohlberg acknowledges that this undoubtedly represents a violation of (one form of) the naturalistic fallacy. It is, however, a violation that he is prepared to countenance.

A further aspect of Kohlberg's theory is the mode of communication that takes place in what he terms the "moral judgment interview" between research scientist and interviewee. Wishing to characterize such interaction as a "dialogue" — indeed as a hermeneutic dialogue[24] — Kohlberg tells us that "when doing interpretative social science one must enter with an attitude of communication between the observer and the observed; that is, one must 'join a conversation'" (218). What is meant by "joining a conversation," however, is not a recognition that the interviewee may understand truths not already comprehended by the researcher, and that the latter may thus have something to learn from the former. Because the interviewee has the status not of an interlocutor on an equal footing with the interviewer but of a research

subject, Kohlberg's "hermeneutic dialogue" is in no relevant respect different from clinical diagnosis. Dialogue, he writes, includes
the employment of "a standardized issue scoring manual and a
standardized interview for assessing moral reasoning" (219).
Kohlberg and his colleagues have developed a measurement technique that "we believe allows us to have our psychometric cake
and hermeneutically interpret it too" (219). The interview process
begins with the researcher endeavoring to occupy the moral standpoint of the research subject. (Since the interviewer has progressed
through each moral stage, there is no difficulty in transposing oneself into the standpoint of any moral agent, regardless of which
developmental stage the latter occupies.) The interviewer then proceeds to "score" the interviewee's responses to standardized questions. What Kohlberg characterizes as a hermeneutic approach in
his investigations is one in which dialogue is not an interpretive
art but a (quasi-) science.

By incorporating Kohlberg's moral psychology into a more encompassing theory of individual and societal development, Habermas rehabilitates historical materialism and preserves the standing
of critical theory as a scientific, historically oriented analysis of
the present. The theory of social evolution provides a framework
not only from which to measure the moral competence of individuals, but from which to explain the deep significance of social
phenomena and for the critique of social conditions past and present. It reinstates critical theory's claim to scientific status by viewing present conditions as stages in maturational processes and social
conflicts as developmental problems. It offsets the potentially conservative and relativistic effects of the recognition of historicity
by viewing criticism as a mode of scientific knowledge derived
from the standpoint of an end-state of integrated learning processes.
It is from this theoretical vantage point that social criticism may
assess the practices and norms that have generated consensus not
only in modern Western societies but indeed in any culture and

any historical period. The reconstruction of historical materialism thus provides a new foundation for emancipatory critique.

The Ideal of Scientificity

I argued in chapter two that tensions in Foucault's critique of power are traceable to his genealogical conception of critique. This method of criticism, by refusing to occupy any particular normative standpoint, leaves the critic without the resources necessary for such reflection and leaves Foucault silent where we should least expect it. Habermas, on the other hand, not only identifies but provides a transcendental grounding for the standpoint from which the critique of ideology proceeds. Critique, as a dimension of explanatory science, is practiced from the scientific standpoint of an end-state of developmental processes. By bringing together normative evaluation and scientific knowledge, Habermas provides a systematic grounding for social criticism. Critical theory thus acknowledges its historical emergence while preserving a claim to scientific objectivity by conceiving history as a configuration of developmental processes leading toward a condition of superior communicative and interactive competence.

While clearly not vulnerable to the criticisms directed above against Foucaultian genealogy, Habermas's transcendental project is not without difficulties of its own — difficulties that stem from his conception of critique as a mode of scientific investigation. A few of these difficulties were alluded to in our discussion of Foucault and his critique of the science/ideology opposition in Marxism. They are given a different interpretation by Hans-Georg Gadamer in the course of his debate with Habermas. While Habermas has changed the focus of his thought since the time of the debate with Gadamer from psychoanalysis and self-reflection to the reconstruction of historical materialism, this change of focus does not constitute a change in position. In his more recent writings,

Habermas remains as committed as ever to the ideal of scientificity and to conceiving social criticism in terms of the science/ideology opposition. The search for a theoretical frame of reference from which to comprehend society as a totality and to detect the deep meaning of social phenomena in the manner of psychoanalysis remains at the center of Habermas's concerns. This is the focus of Gadamer's rejoinder to Habermas in the course of their debate. Our question is whether this line of criticism remains relevant after Habermas's turn toward competence theory.

Among the questions at stake in this well-known debate is whether critical theory can transcend the situation-dependency of hermeneutic interpretation by employing the methods of psychoanalysis. Can normative criticism achieve the status of a science?[25] We have seen how Habermas has undertaken to answer this question in the affirmative by modeling the emancipatory aim of the critic and the method of diagnosing communal neuroses on the practice of psychoanalysis. The mode of communication between critic and society is similarly patterned after the clinical interaction between analyst and analysand in the therapeutic dialogue.

In psychoanalysis, the authority of the analyst is contingent on the following conditions: first, feelings of unhappiness and frustration on the part of the patient; second, the analyst's knowledge of the causes of these feelings; third, the patient's recognition of the analyst's knowledge; fourth, the analyst being exempt from neurotic disturbances. The significance of the fourth condition goes back to Freud's insistence that before one practices psychoanalysis one must oneself undergo analysis in order to be free of the disturbances one is later to diagnose in others. Regarding the second condition, the analyst must be capable of explaining the sufferings of patients as frustrations of their true interests. The analyst must not only comprehend the meaning of patients' expressions better than they themselves do, but know as well the real needs and interests of the patients. Because the patients are in the grip of an illusion, they fail to understand their real interests just as they fail to understand themselves. The third condition — that the asymmetry in the relation of doctor and patient is contingent on the latter's free recognition of the authority and superior knowledge of the psychoanalyst — is also indispensable. The authoritative status and the pedagogical role of the analyst are both defused when the analysand refuses the subordinate position of patient in a clinical mode of interaction.

The question thus arises whether these conditions hold in the interaction between social critic and society, as it would seem they must for Habermas's analogy to hold. Regarding the first condition — that the authority of the analyst in the therapeutic dialogue must presuppose feelings of frustration on the part of the analysand (who, needless to say, would not undergo treatment were it not for such feelings) — a problem arises: what happens in the event that individuals or social groups are so under the spell of ideology that they do not experience their position in the social order as oppressive? If the illusions that hold them captive are so essential to their self-understanding that they do not experience their frustrations as in any way abnormal or oppressive — if such feelings are explainable within an ideological worldview and accepted as part of the natural order of things — a necessary condition of the analyst/critic's authority does not hold. The very individuals and groups most in need of critical self-consciousness will hear the claims of the critic (beginning with the claim that the latter occupies a superior position in detecting real meanings and real interests) with deaf ears. The scenario in which persons are in the grip of an illusion to such a degree is far from hypothetical if we grant Freud's thesis that neuroses may afflict not only whole communities but nearly all of humankind. If we grant as well Freud's belief that religion represents the universal neurosis of humankind, then the scenario is not even unusual.

The second condition — the authority claimed by the analyst in the therapeutic dialogue — is the focus of Gadamer's criticism. For the critic of ideology to claim a superior perspective prior to participating in dialogue with other social agents, including those whom the critic holds to be victims of false consciousness, is the worst form of dogmatism. As Gadamer expresses it, "How does the psychoanalyst's special knowledge relate to his own position within the societal reality (to which, after all, he does belong)? The psychoanalyst leads the patient into the emancipatory reflection that goes behind the conscious superficial interpretations, breaks through the masked self-understanding, and sees through the repressive function of social taboos. This activity belongs to the emancipatory reflection to which he leads his patient. But what happens when he uses the same kind of reflection in a situation in which he is not the doctor but a partner in a game? Then he will fall out of his social role! A game partner who is always 'seeing through' his game partner, who does not take seriously what they are standing for, is a spoil sport whom one shuns."[26] Habermas's ideology critic pretends already to know the outcome of rational dialogue before it has begun, to be in sole possession of the truth while the claims of interlocutors are dismissed as illusions. Exempting the critic's conception of justice from the need for dialogue with others omits the simple possibilities of difference of opinion and of learning from opposed viewpoints. The danger that would arise should this radically nonegalitarian mode of communication be transferred to the domain of politics may be readily discerned: individuals, presuming to know the interests of others better than they themselves, would constitute no small menace were they to find their way into positions of power. Refusing to grant that the values of their would-be interlocutors may have some claim to legitimacy, such persons are likely to impose their political agenda upon everyone within their reach.

Habermas's response to this line of criticism is to distinguish three tasks of political discourse. First, the task of theory construction; second, the organization of enlightenment; and third, the conduct of political struggle. Theory construction imposes no constraints on communication. The position of all speakers is equal, and the course of inquiry is determined solely by the force of the strongest argument. The third task is characterized as a search for consensus among social actors struggling for emancipation concerning the strategic actions most likely to achieve their aims. It is only within the organization of enlightenment that speakers occupy asymmetrical positions on the therapeutic model. This is the pedagogical communication between critic and society, the legitimacy of which rests on the superior knowledge of the former. Since the practice of enlightening individuals and groups about their predicament within the social order neither requires nor entails that any specific actions be undertaken, since it offers no positive recommendations regarding how such groups must secure their emancipation, Habermas argues that the danger of the enlighteners dogmatically imposing their values on the rest of the population does not arise.

Does this separation of functions suffice as a reply to Gadamer? Has Habermas's turn toward competence theory since this debate made his position less vulnerable to the same objection? I suggest that both questions be answered in the negative for the following reasons. The aim of social criticism is to enlighten those in need of emancipation; it is identified, in other words, with the second task above and not the third. Habermas apparently supposes that the dogmatism to which Gadamer objects would pose a danger only if practiced in the conduct of political struggle where questions of strategic action arise, and that no such danger exists at the level of the organization of enlightenment. We need not worry about new impositions of power since it is not the task of the enlighteners to prescribe which direction the political struggle must take. However, it is not only at the level of political struggle that the problem of dogmatism arises. The social critic who pronounces verdicts in a dialogical vacuum, who claims special authority by virtue of special insight, resorts to a form of dogmatism that creates a new class structure in the practice of political communication.

This immunization of one set of values from conversation is

perpetuated by Habermas's turn toward Kohlbergian competence theory. Let us recall for a moment the mode of communication that takes place in Kohlberg's moral judgment interview between analyst and research subject. In this conversation, after listening to and "scoring" the latter's responses to a set of standardized questions, the analyst/scientist/critic proceeds to inform the interviewee of the latter's level of competence as a moral deliberator. (It goes without saying that the latter does not enjoy the same privilege.) It is by virtue of the knowledge of what constitutes superior moral competence that the scientist enjoys the same authority in the moral judgment interview as the psychoanalyst in therapeutic dialogue. Thus, to the individual at the highest level of moral competence, dialogue with those at the conventional and preconventional levels (some 80 percent of the population of American adults) does not involve listening to the claims of an interlocutor with the recognition that such claims may be legitimate; it is a means of gaining information about the competence level of the moral agents in question, just as psychoanalytic interaction is a form not of listening to but of "seeing through" the utterances of a disturbed patient. The result is a new conversational regime involving a class of speakers claiming authority by virtue of superior competence and an underclass of all the rest.

As we have seen, Kohlberg asserts that if his developmental approach to moral competence is sound, it follows that "the only 'competent moral speakers' are the rare individuals at Stage 6 (or, more tolerantly, at Stages 6 and 5)." Kohlberg also asserts that if we wish to ascertain the normative status of a given practice, "we need only ascertain its moral status among people who are in the vanguard, so to speak, of moral development in our society." It is odd that Habermas, an outspoken defender of unconstrained communication, who from his earliest writings has been concerned with rehabilitating the notion of the public sphere as a forum wherein all speakers may engage in dialogue about matters of general interest, and who professes the "conviction that a humane collective

life depends on the vulnerable forms of innovation-bearing, reciprocal and unforcedly egalitarian everyday communication," would
attribute such import to a theory that legitimizes a new class structure of moral agents.[27]

Habermas and Kohlberg have both retreated from positing
"hard" stages at the postconventional level of moral reasoning. Both
now maintain that once moral agents advance beyond stage four
they reach the level of reflective moral consciousness. Accordingly,
the asymmetry between speakers is replaced at the postconventional
level by (relative) equality between (relatively) competent moral
agents. As Habermas writes, "[T]he relationship of psychologist
to interviewee in the interview situation has to change as soon as
the subject reaches the formal-operational or postconventional level
of thought or moral judgment. For at this level the asymmetry that
exists in preceding stages between the subject's prereflective efforts and the psychologist's attempt to grasp them reflectively disappears. And with this, the cognitive discrepancy that was originally
built into the interview situation disappears."[28] However, it is still
only those at stages five and six (now characterized as "soft" stages)
who possess sufficient moral judgment to be capable of dialogue
in the proper sense of the term. The normative claims of those at
lower developmental stages are not to be reflected upon with an
eye to their possible legitimacy, they are to be "tallied" with the
aid of Kohlberg's standard issue scoring manual. Gadamer's charge
of dogmatism, accordingly, carries still more force after Habermas's
Kohlbergian turn than at the time of their debate.

A second line of argument advanced by Gadamer also has equal
or greater force after Habermas's turn toward developmental theory.
This line of criticism concerns the notion of self-reflection. Gadamer charges that the claims that Habermas makes on behalf of self-
reflection are excessive and overlook the partiality and facticity of
all inquiry. Recalling that one of the basic aims of critical theory
is to offset what it regards as the conservative and relativistic effects
of maintaining, in the manner of philosophical hermeneutics, that

all discourse is situated within tradition and language, Habermas proposes that it is through self-reflection that a critical social science may detect the workings of ideology. In introducing a measure of objectivity into the analysis of social phenomena, self-reflection offsets the situatedness of hermeneutic interpretation. To this, Gadamer objects that Habermas's notion of self-reflection constitutes a thorough misunderstanding of the way in which social phenomena are comprehended. Specifically, it overlooks the extent to which reflection is already preceded by tacit understandings. Human consciousness is never in the entirely sovereign position of absolute distance from its object, but is symbolically mediated and embedded within an ontological preunderstanding. To suppose that through self-reflection social critics could get behind language to its "real" determinants is to misrepresent language as a mere adjunct of social reality rather than the universal medium through which phenomena are brought into view. While ostensibly recognizing the conditionedness of reflection, Habermas defends a conception of social criticism that overlooks its proper limits, and for this reason appears to constitute yet another form of totalizing reflection.

What Habermas overlooks in particular is the embeddedness of critique within tradition and particular horizons of reflection. Although the aim of his transcendental project is to release criticism from the workings of tradition, to disengage critical theory from its facticity, Habermas loses sight of the tradition in which his own ethical thought is situated. As Ricoeur points out, Habermas's project stands within what he terms a tradition of emancipation.

> For in the end, hermeneutics will say, from where do you speak when you appeal to *Selbstreflexion*, if it is not from the place that you yourself have denounced as a non-place, the non-place of the transcendental subject? It is indeed from the basis of a tradition that you speak. This tradition is not perhaps the same as Gadamer's; it is perhaps that of the *Aufklärung*, whereas Gadamer's would be Romanticism. But it is a tradition nonetheless, the tradition of emancipation rather than that of recollection. Critique is also a tradition. I would even say that it plunges into the most impressive tradition,

that of liberating acts, of the Exodus and the Resurrection. Perhaps there would be no more interest in emancipation, no more anticipation of freedom, if the Exodus and the Resurrection were effaced from the memory of mankind.[29]

It is in the context of a tradition of emancipation stemming from Judaism and Christianity, then to the Enlightenment, Kantianism, Marxism, and so on, that the critique of ideology gains intelligibility. The basic aims, categories, and assumptions it employs both in justifying and opposing existing practice are all found within this tradition. Far from gaining transcendental insight into historical traditions, ideology critique is itself situated within tradition, the claims of self-reflection notwithstanding.

By the same token, Habermas's turn toward evolutionary and competence theory, rather than providing a distanced, tradition-neutral perspective on present forms of reasoning, is properly viewed in light of the Kantian moral tradition. As Kohlberg acknowledges, his developmental psychology is by no means ethically neutral, but is premised on modern formalist and deontological moral philosophy stemming from Kant. In view of this, Kohlberg's theory of moral competence is improperly conceived as a scientific discourse demonstrating empirically the true normative status of our practices and reasonings; it is a partisan endeavor deriving the kind of judgments one would expect given the assumptions built into it. It is no accident that the culmination of moral development to Kohlberg bears a striking resemblance to the dutiful follower of the categorical imperative. As Foucault might say, Kohlbergian moral psychology is in fact plain old Kantian morality in the guise of scientific knowledge, awarding privileged status to one normative standpoint by concealing its perspectivity and installing it atop a scientific hierarchy of knowledges.

While acknowledging the circularity of Kohlberg's view that ethical principles can be corroborated by a scientific theory itself informed by ethical assumptions, Habermas insists that this circularity is not vicious. The relation between moral philosophy and developmental psychology, as mentioned above, is one of mutual reinforcement, with each providing corroboration of the other's conclusions. The operative criterion here is coherence: when moral judgments cohere with the findings of developmental psychology, such judgments are well grounded. It is through the combination of "*several* theoretical spotlights"[30] that critical reflection may claim scientific objectivity. The problem with this position is twofold: first, the circularity in question is vicious because the formal principles Kohlberg's theory presents as the culmination of moral competence are justified by formalist assumptions. There is nothing scientifically interesting in the discovery that Kantian conclusions follow from Kantian premises. Second, and more fundamentally, it is far from obvious why moral reflection requires the confirmation of empirical science. Even (or perhaps especially) if we approach the question from within Kohlberg's own frame of reference and regard the domain of morality, as he suggests, as a "unique *sui generis* realm" of discourse, one in which normative claims are judged solely by normative criteria, it is not clear why such claims should need justification by empirical science. As Foucault might ask, what special dignity is it to convey the title of scientific respectability on normative judgments? Is the ideal of scientificity so insisted on by critical theory not merely a prejudice of modernity — one that, far from transcending the contingency of historical tradition, in fact reveals the extent of critical theory's participation in the modern Enlightenment tradition? Does it conceal the workings of a particular power/knowledge configuration characteristic of modernity? Again, a Foucaultian reading suggests itself.

In sum, both genealogical and (quasi-)scientific practices of critique raise formidable difficulties. While genealogy leaves us with a limited capacity for reasoned criticism on account of its refusal to identify the standpoint from which it speaks, critical theory makes excessive claims regarding its status, and at times deteriorates into a new form of dogmatism. The twin dangers to which these views give rise are, first, the lack of philosophical rationality that can be claimed for criticism that occurs from no apparent perspective and, second, the dogmatism associated with transcendental and scientific perspectives. If we are in search of a standpoint for the critique of power, we must avoid the twin dangers of speaking from a place which is no-place and speaking from a totalizing perspective. If social criticism is to maintain a degree of historical consciousness, it is imperative that it abandon the search for a privileged standpoint. We must, in short, find a better way of reconciling our historicity with the need for critique.

Four

The Practice of Criticism

*T*he practice of criticism involves more than deriving conclusions from premises. It involves the interpretation of meaning and an appropriation of a moral language and tradition. The preoccupation with deduction has traditionally led philosophers to overlook both the hermeneutic dimension of criticism and the implication of its categories within contingent horizons and power structures. The fascination with technique has led mainline theorists to overlook the extent to which critique has always already brought its object into view in a manner that is far from neutral. It has already interpreted the significance of its object from the perspective not of "morality as such" but of a particular normative standpoint, a horizon of tacit evaluations and preunderstandings which simultaneously precedes, makes possible, and limits reflection. In investigating the "always already" of critique, the textual character of human action, and the nature of practical judgment, we can see that critique is an essentially hermeneutic mode of reflection. This line of argument serves to correct fundamental and common misconceptions about the practice of criticism.

Drawing primarily on the work of Gadamer and Ricoeur, I argue in this chapter that human action is a text analogue, the significance of which is contingent on the interpretive framework of the critic.

This argument challenges notions of rational and scientific objectivity operative in several methods of normative theorizing, including critical theory. Understanding critique as a hermeneutic practice allows us to incorporate what is of value in the thought of Nietzsche, Foucault, and Habermas while surpassing the limitations of genealogy and avoiding the excesses of ideology critique. An adequate account of social criticism must identify the vantage point from which it speaks without appealing to totalizing perspectives, and incorporate an attitude of suspicion without sacrificing the capacity for affirmation. The practice of criticism is dialectical. Situated within a particular ethical-political horizon — a perspective constituted by values and categories appropriated from tradition and by theoretically generated principles — critical reflection seeks the remediation of social ills by disclosing new possibilities of meaning. Through hermeneutic redescription and practical judgment, social criticism brings to light dimensions of meaning that habitual ways of speaking conceal. Developing this view leads into a broader discussion of moral imagination, the hermeneutics of suspicion, and *phronesis*. The hermeneutical conception of critique as a dialectic of recollection and innovation, tradition and reform, universal and particular, provides a response to Habermas's allegation that hermeneutics leaves us with an attenuated capacity for critical reflection or an unreflective conservatism. As long as semantic innovation, imaginative redescription, hermeneutic dialogue, and practical judgment remain, critical reflection is possible.

The Facticity of Critique

To engage in criticism is always already to have conveyed intelligibility upon an object of reflection. One has taken an object into view, integrated it within a conceptual framework, and interpreted its significance. One cannot evaluate what one has not first understood.

The reason criticism must include a hermeneutic component

is found in the nature of the object of criticism itself, namely human conduct. To be rendered intelligible (or sufficiently intelligible for the purpose of criticism), human action is not adequately characterized in empirical or causal terms. An adequate rendering must incorporate that which makes it a specifically human phenomenon, namely its significance. Understanding action means conceiving it as meaningfully oriented behavior (to borrow an expression of Max Weber's), a meaning that is underdetermined in that there is always a variety of potentially salient features in terms of which its significance may be understood. To take an example: when the President sends in the troops, he or she may be protecting national security, building an empire, diverting attention from the domestic scene, enlightening the heretic, triggering global conflict, making the world safe for democracy, or all of the above. Meaning may be disclosed in the intention of the agent, something inherent to the action itself (a maxim), or the consequences (intended or unintended) for the agent or others. Which feature is salient to understanding is not given. This is to say with Ricoeur that human action is a "text analogue," in that much the same hermeneutic efforts involved in reading a text enter into the interpretation of conduct. Action is autonomous with respect to its agent just as a text is autonomous with respect to its author.[1] Lacking a determinate significance, action, once taken up into discourse, escapes its agent and becomes subject to competing interpretations. Thus, in sending in the troops, the President's intention to protect human rights may be overshadowed by the triggering of global conflict, an unintended and perhaps unforeseeable consequence. Given that criticism presupposes an understanding of its object, we need to know the conditions of the possibility of understanding itself, since these conditions are fundamental to the practice of criticism. This question is central to Heideggerian and Gadamerian hermeneutics.

Heidegger demonstrates in *Being and Time* that thematic understanding is subsequent to being-in-the-world, an expression connoting involvement in a meaningful totality of relations, a world both encompassing and largely presupposed. The human being is "thrown" into a network of involvements and understandings within which it gains a fundamental orientation. While being-in-the-world is always marked by a tacit understanding, explicit comprehension requires an act of interpretation. This involves the introduction of the hermeneutical "as." To interpret something is to view it as a particular kind of thing or in the light of a concept. An action, for instance, is interpreted as belonging to a certain practice or manner of behavior.

Interpretation involves an anticipatory projection of significa-tion associated with what Heidegger calls the "forestructure" of understanding. An object's mode of being is constituted by a prior framework of understanding in which phenomena are compre-hended. Reflection never attains absolute distance from its object since it is preceded and made possible by tacit understandings that orient us to phenomena in particular ways. Consciousness inhabits a lifeworld or ethos antecedent to all explicit assertion and evalua-tion. Our hermeneutic standpoint is one that we neither stand out-side of nor grasp in its totality, but is something of which we can gain only partial awareness. The perspectivity that makes under-standing possible also constitutes a limit for understanding.

Heidegger's anchoring of interpretation within an ontological preunderstanding is taken up in Gadamer's *Truth and Method*, no-tably in the latter's hypothesis concerning the prejudicial character of interpretation. In opposition to the Enlightenment ideal of pre-suppositionless apprehension, Gadamer maintains that reflection, no matter how dispassionate or meticulous, presupposes a set of tacit judgments, many of which escape our notice and are accepted uncritically. Reflection is simultaneously preceded, made possible, and limited by prereflective and often unconscious background judgments against which phenomena come into view. A prejudice, Gadamer writes, is "a judgment that is rendered before all the ele-ments that determine a situation have been finally examined." It constitutes not a false or irrational belief but the initial directedness of reflection and an anticipatory disclosure. Against the view that prejudice merely imprisons us in dogmatism, Gadamer argues that prejudices, while biases, "are biases of our openness to the world. They are simply conditions whereby we experience something — whereby what we encounter says something to us." The prejudices at work in interpretation have their origin not in arbitrary subjectivity but in historical tradition. They are historical constructs — judgments that have become tacit and receded into the background of consciousness. This is the meaning of Gadamer's claim that the human being "belongs" to history. "In fact history does not belong to us; we belong to it. Long before we understand ourselves through the process of self-examination, we understand ourselves in a self-evident way in the family, society, and state in which we live. The focus of subjectivity is a distorting mirror. The self-awareness of the individual is only a flickering in the closed circuits of historical life. *That is why the prejudices of the individual, far more than his judgments, constitute the historical reality of his being.*"[2]

Gadamer's view of subjectivity as an historical construction is inseparable from his claim that consciousness always finds itself situated within tradition. Rather than conceiving tradition as something that is essentially over and done with — an object behind us which we can either assent to or reject as a whole — Gadamer conceives of tradition as a conversation. Tradition exists only in mediation with the present and is inseparable from its manner of appropriation. A genuine participation in historical tradition is neither a simple repetition of the past nor an abdication of rationality. While traditions often succumb to dogmatism, their proper nature is to exist in perpetual reconstitution. Living traditions persist not out of inertia but through free appropriation and creative transformation. Gadamer thus opposes both romantic and Enlightenment thinkers who regarded tradition and reason as standing in mutual opposition.[3] While the claims that traditions make on us are subject to rational assessment, such assessment is part of what it means to belong to a tradition rather than a complete distancing from the past.

These premises are not without consequence for an understanding of normative criticism since they bring to light the historicity of moral consciousness. If all reflection is situated within a tradition or horizon of historically contingent prejudices, criticism is not only limited but made possible by prereflective judgments. It proceeds not in presuppositionless fashion but against a background of tacit evaluations and partial descriptions which provide an initial orientation to social reality. Moral consciousness is never in the position of neutral spectator on human affairs; it has already been preceded by prejudice.

Another premise of hermeneutics is that interpretation occurs in language, since it is language that furnishes interpretation with the categories in light of which phenomena are disclosed, namely as instances of a certain kind of thing. To understand something explicitly is to incorporate it within a linguistic framework. Understanding is not prelinguistic and articulated afterwards in language. We gain an understanding precisely when we find the words that allow us to speak of an object. The hermeneutical conception of language as *"the universal medium in which understanding occurs"*[4] contrasts with the view of language as a tool to manipulate at will and set aside after it has served its purpose. There is an intimacy between reflection and language that is overlooked in viewing language as an object attached to understanding *ex post facto*.

Like Heidegger's Being, language is not a reified entity but a medium of disclosure, "the medium in which we live from the outset as social natures and which holds open the totality within which we live our lives."[5] As the standpoint and medium of reflection, language does not permit complete distancing in the sense of being a potentially unified object of reflection. Nor is it merely a collection of signs and rules of syntax. Language is primarily speech, a saying that discloses particulars in the light of universals. As speech, language remains largely hidden from view since what is visible to consciousness is not language itself but the phenomena that make their appearance in language.[6] Herein lies a special problem for interpretation. As Gadamer writes: "The interpreter does not know that he is bringing himself and his own concepts into the interpretation. The verbal formulation is so much part of the interpreter's mind that he never becomes aware of it as an object."[7] We overlook the extent of our involvement in interpretation, mistaking a contingent mode of access for presuppositionless observation. The extent of the social critic's involvement in moral perception is often similarly overlooked. It is often imagined that by means of theory construction social criticism could ascend to a place called "the moral point of view," a standpoint from which complete distancing from practices and tradition is possible. In imagining this, the very conditions of normative reflection — its essential perspectivity, historicity, and linguisticality — are lost sight of. To practice criticism is already to have interpreted the significance of an object by means of the hermeneutical "as," and from the standpoint of an historical tradition; it is to have taken an object into view in the light of prejudices, many of which are tacit evaluations.

In addition, critique invariably adopts a particular moral language and involves the same process of linguistic assimilation that characterizes interpretation.[8] As recent work in moral philosophy has brought out, it no longer makes sense to speak as if there were a single language of morality.[9] There are distinct normative vocabularies organized around different concepts and whose claims upon us are of entirely different kinds. There is the vocabulary of human rights, virtue, utility, care, honor, sin and redemption, and so on. Each vocabulary constitutes a manner of experiencing and comporting oneself toward social reality. To speak a moral language is to adopt a perspective on social practices, to appropriate a way of life, and to bear an identity as a moral agent. To speak the language of utility, for instance, is to be a certain kind of moral agent and to experience social reality in ways quite different from one who appropriates the language of sin and redemption.

A normative vocabulary directs reflection in particular ways and informs what we are likely to perceive as the salient features of moral action. Moral perception is no simple apprehension of what presents itself to the unclouded eye, but selects which features of a case are of special relevance for interpretation. The moral language spoken crucially affects the identification of saliences, the articulation of significance, and hence the judgment that is fashioned. It is thus far from trivial which moral language social criticism adopts precisely because the vocabulary it speaks always bespeaks the phenomena in a particular (non-neutral) way. This view of the disclosive (or, as Heidegger would say, the "unconcealing") nature of language leads to an intimacy of language and reflection.

Thus we must abandon conceptions of critique as an objective, presuppositionless, or aperspectival mode of discourse. We cannot rid ourselves of normative presuppositions and, as one author expresses it, "gaze directly into the Moral Law, using it as a standard for judging the justification or truth of moral propositions, any more than [we] can gaze directly into the mind of God." The necessity of reflecting from where we are rules out the possibility of "having your judgment determined solely by the matter under consideration without relying on beliefs, habits of description, and patterns of reasoning that belong to a cultural inheritance."[10] It rules out not only the possibility of totalizing reflection but the myths of moral expertise and the moral point of view (a single standpoint from which to practice criticism). It gives further reason to abandon the ideal of scientificity and the science/ideology opposition. For critical reflection to be properly self-critical, it must forget neither its conditions of possibility nor its limits.

Understanding the practice of criticism begins with a recognition of its facticity. Criticism is always *in medias res*, working against the background of a shared way of life. While it is clear that normative discourse is characterized by dissent, contestation itself (when it is meaningful, or when persons do not merely talk past one another) presupposes what Gadamer calls a "deep common accord."[11] In mediating disagreements, we typically appeal not to supposed moral facts but to beliefs not currently in question, judgments concerning what is valuable given our shared self-understanding and common participation in a lifeworld.

This Gadamerian line of argument is often taken as an invitation to conservatism. Habermas in particular (as we have seen) charges that the accent hermeneutics places on facticity creates a prejudice in favor of current practice and undermines the emancipatory intent of critical reflection. This objection deserves to be taken seriously. While critique occurs from where we are, its role is not only to preserve current practice (or those practices that are worthy of preservation), but to challenge, illuminate, and reform. A satisfactory account of this practice must reconcile the critic's involvement in tradition and existing power structures with the capacity for opposition. Historical belonging does not imply captivity. That critique never gains total distance from its object does not negate the possibility of every social and discursive practice, every morally interesting action and institution becoming an object of criticism. While there is no vantage point from which social reality can be criticized as a totality, every element of social life may be subjected to critical appraisal, albeit not simultaneously.

Critical Hermeneutics and Moral Imagination

Drawing attention to the "always already" of critique is not an invitation to conservatism but a reminder of the conditions and limits of reflection. The problem of conservatism arises only if facticity is viewed not as one moment of social criticism but as its only moment. Critical reflection is dialectical in structure, the two moments of which are what Ricoeur calls factual recollection and semantic innovation. Historically situated, critique proceeds by recollecting what is handed down through tradition. Yet it is able to extend the horizon that it occupies by creating new avenues of disclosure and remaining open to difference. Critical hermeneutics can call into question the meaning that social phenomena have for us on the basis of our being-in-the-world.

The practice of criticism is profoundly misconceived when recollection and innovation, tradition and reform, are viewed as antithetical. While moral consciousness is oriented by tradition, it is able to modify perceptions through an imaginative application of language. A hermeneutical conception of critique renounces the myth of total enlightenment and views critique as opening up new dimensions of meaning, revealing what habitual understandings conceal and transforming what is given into what is questionable. It is largely the innovative dimension of critique — the capacity for imaginative redescription — that introduces an attitude of suspicion toward existing practice.

While imagination is conventionally conceived as the capacity to fashion images, Ricoeur argues that this overlooks what is most essential to imagination: its linguistic dimension and connection with the as-structure of interpretation. Imagination is properly conceived as a linguistic capacity that responds to the need for original signification, for loosening the hold of habitual ways of understanding, by differently categorizing particulars. New meaning emerges when a different conceptuality is brought to bear on phenomena. Imagination is the capacity to modify perception and extend the limits of understanding by revealing new possibilities of interpretation.[12]

The moral imagination is traditionally conceived as the psychological capacity to transpose oneself into the standpoint of other agents — to "put ourselves in the minds of other men" as Kant expressed it — and to perceive our actions from their perspectives. This view overlooks the manner in which moral imagination invests social reality with significance and fashions creative interpretations of human action. It is better regarded as the capacity by which moral perception is modified by means of novel and potentially illuminating description. Moral imagination involves perceiving an action from the standpoint of both different agents and different concepts — seeing it, for instance, as an act of friendship and generosity or as one of pity and condescension. By questioning habitual significations, it reveals the contingency behind all supposed moral facts, revealing that behind the apparent givenness of our perceptions is only one possible application of the hermeneutical "as."

Ricoeur points out that it is the polysemic character of concepts that makes imaginative signification possible. Words in natural language are underdetermined in their meaning, and this ambiguity makes it possible to view phenomena under different descriptions. This can be seen most clearly in the case of symbolic (particularly religious and poetic) language, but the categories of social criticism also contain semantic ambiguity. Moral imagination illuminates action anew by subsuming it under a different conceptuality, an interpretive act made possible by the polysemy of normative concepts. Far from eliminating ambiguity altogether, understanding a moral concept involves preserving and explicating several different, yet related, significations, noting similarities in its applications without reducing it to a univocal expression. We can say of moral concepts what Ricoeur says of symbols — that "to reflect upon these symbols and to interpret them is one and the same act."[13]

To illustrate: we may critique an action by designating it as a transgression or violation. Novel signification introduces an attitude of suspicion that calls into question our received view of the action's significance and moral status. Thus we might designate as oppressive what had been viewed as an act of altruism. Yet the concepts of oppression, violation, and transgression resist encapsulation within univocal expressions. While in many instances it is not difficult to identify examples and applications of a moral concept, identification of its "essential" meaning eludes us. Although philosophers typically regard polysemy as a formula for misunderstanding, it is important to emphasize that the polysemy of moral concepts is an essential condition of moral imagination. The elasticity of concepts makes it possible to reform established idiom and thus modify perception. Were the meaning of normative concepts to be captured within exhaustive definitions, clarity of thought would be purchased at the price of a severe impairment of the capacity for criticism.

One means by which moral imagination modifies perception is through metaphor. Ricoeur builds on Aristotle's notion of metaphor as "an intuitive perception of the similarity in dissimilars"[14] and a bringing together of formerly disparate semantic fields, a process that allows the interpreter to "get hold of something fresh" (1410b). New meaning emerges through what Ricoeur calls "*impertinent predication*," an apprehension of new resemblance made possible by a relating of previously unrelated terms.[15] The same reintegration of semantic fields characterizes the practice of criticism. Perceptions are modified when a given action is likened to another — when, for instance, an action is viewed in proximity to another which is deemed unjust. When "property is theft" and politics is "war by other means," a moral context is perceived in a new and potentially suggestive light.

In relating hitherto disparate terms, imaginative predication transcends established meaning by "misusing" language as it is habitually understood. While operating within an established order of language, metaphor fashions new meaning by creating a breach in this order. The transference of meaning from one conceptual domain to another is not only a borrowing of terminology but a transgression of boundaries and a violation of the normal functioning of language. Metaphorical language redescribes by reclassifying; in "mistaking," as it were, one thing for another, it extends the literal meaning of concepts and reforms existing systems of classification.[16] Through a disruption of the old order, a new linguistic order is created, one in which it becomes possible for the first time to express what had been not only unexpressed but unexpressible. It becomes intelligible to speak of history as a class struggle, civilization as repression of desire, and morality as will to power. Although Ricoeur incorporates Aristotle's view of metaphor as an apprehension of similarity in dissimilars, such similarity is not antecedently present in the terms that metaphor brings into proximity. The likenesses that imagination brings to light are constituted in the act of predication. To speak of resemblance is thus to speak of a proximity in semantic space. "[R]esemblance itself," Ricoeur writes, "must be understood as a tension between identity and difference in the predicative operation set in motion by semantic innovation."[17] The "perception of the similarity in dissimilars" is a perception that invents rather than discovers.

Imagination, accordingly, is a capacity for synthesizing the heterogeneous. As Ricoeur argues, this act of synthesis, or semantic innovation, characterizes not only metaphorical predication but narrative as well. The meaning of an action is understood not only when it is subsumed under a universal but when it is emplotted in a narrative. Understanding the President's order to send in the troops involves seeing the action as belonging to a narrative: a continuation of traditional policy, a chapter in the political biography of a president, or a catalyst for global conflict. Comprehending its meaning involves viewing the action not as an isolated occurrence but in proximity to other actions — as a prelude, a response, a departure, or a consequence of other events. By emplotting actions within a narrative structure, it is possible to "grasp together" an assortment of events, intentions, and consequences which all contribute to an action's significance.

The reason narrative is essential to the understanding of action lies in the nature of action as temporal and meaningfully oriented behavior, that is, behavior oriented by the past (as a continuation or departure) and toward the future. Action is goal oriented, and while it does not always attain its aim, its aims are invariably present. In interpreting its meaning, we endeavor to identify the agent's intention, even when, as is often the case, the intention is unarticulated, confused, several in number, or conflicting. The sense of an action, however, is not reducible to its intention. Its actual consequences are as significant (in many cases more so) as its intended consequences. Our actions are never a perfect embodiment of our aims, and because unintended consequences are often of far-reaching importance, such outcomes are plainly relevant to the sense of an action.

Narrative defines the action by "grasping together" such heterogeneous elements as motive, unintended consequences, and the character of the agent. Narrative is essential to criticism since placing an action in a context and comprehending its significance involves viewing it in a temporal sequence. To take an example from fiction: we do not appraise Jean Valjean's act of stealing a loaf of bread in *Les Misérables* without viewing the act in light of the motive of the agent, the circumstances in which it occurred, the character of the man performing it and, decisively in this case, its long-term consequences. Each consideration is kept in view in judging the act's significance and moral status, and it is only within a narrative that this is possible. To characterize the event as a simple act of theft rather than an occasion for personal transformation (hence as a prelude to further action) is to miss the point.[18] Moral imagination gains perspective in describing and redescribing its object, by constructing metaphors and emplotting actions in narratives different from those in which they are habitually understood. By redescribing and retelling, imagination reveals how current perceptions of social reality could be otherwise, and begets an attitude of suspicion toward received understandings.

Under the best of circumstances, critical reflection remains aware that the metaphors and narratives that it constructs, however illuminating, are interpretations. Like interpretations generally, they reveal not the final truth of their object but one among several possible meanings — a meaning, moreover, that conceals other possibilities of interpretation. Yet reflection also has a tendency to idolize its constructions and to mistake a contingent mode of perception for neutral observation. Traditional modes of speech have the potential to harden into dogma, closing themselves off from dissent and demanding conformity. Imagination may also become so enamored with its constructions that, with the passage of time, it forgets how the phenomena that it discloses could ever have been viewed in any other way. Its perceptions become "self-evident" and are transformed into "moral facts." Those who do not perceive the truth of such facts are not seeing differently; they are not seeing at all. They are "morally blind."

Ricoeur observes that metaphors become idols when transformed into literal truths. Their capacity for disclosure is lost when they lose their "event" character:

> In the metaphorical statement . . ., contextual action creates a new meaning which is indeed an event, since it exists only in this particular context; but at the same time, it can be repeated and hence identified as the same. Thus the innovation of an 'emergent meaning' may be regarded as a linguistic creation; but if it is adopted by an influential part of the language community, it may become an everyday meaning and add to the polysemy of lexical entities, contributing thereby to the history of language as code or system. At this final stage, when the meaningful effect that we call metaphor has rejoined the change of meaning which augments polysemy, the metaphor is no longer living but dead. Only authentic, living metaphors are at the same time 'event' *and* 'meaning.'[19]

A part of the meaning that metaphor and narrative bring to light is a function of the "semantic shock" that imaginative signification makes possible. When such significations take hold in a language community, they may themselves become habitual significations and obstacles to reflection, degenerating into clichés which evoke our suspicion and call for new acts of interpretation.[20]

When a social critic envisions alternative possibilities to the prevailing order, or when a movement fashions new metaphors and narratives by which it understands its condition, this imaginative characterization may deteriorate into a new dogma, as needful of demystification as what it replaced. A vocabulary once illuminating may, in gaining currency, begin to conceal more than it reveals. In time its metaphoric constructions are transformed into idols adopted by a movement of believers. Ways of speaking about social reality that are partial descriptions with a history or a genealogy come to pass for the truth because they bore fruit for someone at some time in practice. A vocabulary that captures the imagination may also lose its poignancy when the circumstances in which it was conceived change. A group that regards itself as having occupied a subordinate position in the social order may in time, as circumstances change and as its beliefs take hold, cease to occupy such a position. Its narrative of victimization becomes hackneyed and conceals the plight of other groups who in the meantime have replaced it at the bottom of the social order. Yesterday's insights may be obstacles to reflection today, just as yesterday's liberators may be today's oppressors.

It is the nature of interpretation to disclose and conceal in the same gesture. Symbols and descriptions that take hold in a language community may take hold of it as well. "The revolution," for instance, is a symbol that has made for self-understanding on the part of many modern collectivities and served as a key episode in narratives of liberation. Yet with equal frequency "the revolution" has served to rationalize nearly every injustice imaginable, concealing interests and agendas of every description. If to shed light is also to cast a shadow, it falls to what Ricoeur calls the hermeneutics of suspicion to reveal what present understandings conceal. The three figures whom Ricoeur identifies under the rubric of suspicious hermeneutics — Marx, Nietzsche, and Freud — are one in regarding consciousness as simultaneously a disclosure and a deception. Behind its significations lie the history of class struggle, the will to power, and the repression of desire. While their methods of decipherment vary, hermeneuticists of suspicion all look upon interpretation as a deciphering of the falsifications of consciousness. Each aims to extend the limits of understanding through suspicious interpretation. Ricoeur writes:

What Marx wants is to liberate *praxis* by the understanding of necessity; but this liberation is inseparable from a 'conscious insight'
which victoriously counterattacks the mystification of false consciousness. What Nietzsche wants is the increase of man's power,
the restoration of his force; but the meaning of the will to power
must be recaptured by meditating on the ciphers 'superman,' 'eternal return,' and 'Dionysus,' without which the power in question
would be but worldly violence. What Freud desires is that the one
who is analyzed, by making his own the meaning that was foreign
to him, enlarge his field of consciousness, live better, and finally be
a little freer and, if possible, a little happier. One of the earliest
homages paid to psychoanalysis speaks of 'healing through consciousness.' The phrase is exact — if one means thereby that analysis
wishes to substitute for an immediate and dissimulating consciousness a mediate consciousness taught by the reality principle.[21]

When we regard moral consciousness as both a disclosure and a
deception, it falls to the practice of criticism to investigate what
present evaluations conceal. This entails several things. It means
inquiring into the interests and prejudices that underlie conventional discourse. Involved in this is what Gadamer calls the "testing"
of prejudices. Because "it is the tyranny of hidden prejudices that
makes us deaf to what speaks to us in tradition,"[22] it is necessary to
become aware of and to test prejudices by encountering what is
foreign. In dialogue we may become aware of the hidden presuppositions underlying our evaluations and questions. As Gadamer
observes, it is the question that fashions understanding by establishing presuppositions and setting the parameters within which
interpretation proceeds. When such presuppositions are erroneous,
the question blocks rather than furthers the course of investigation.
The hermeneutics of suspicion, then, must detect the questions at
work in moral discourse and determine whether these are the most
illuminating ones available, or whether they misdirect inquiry. It
may ask, for example, if the question of whether a fetus constitutes
a human being is a suitable way of approaching the abortion issue,
or if such a question leads only to fruitless metaphysical debate. It

must learn as well to see what is worthy of being called into question. An education in suspicion involves learning how to ask questions and to discern what is questionable.

Hermeneutic reflection does not limit itself to intended and explicit meaning, but investigates what remains unarticulated in moral consciousness; as Gadamer writes, "meaning can be experienced even where it is not actually intended."[23] It investigates the ways in which evaluations promote sectarian interests, often under the guise of impartiality. Behind appeals to principle, suspicious hermeneutics uncovers will to power; behind the general will it finds sectarian interests; and behind self-understanding it finds self-misunderstanding. It dissolves the hold such items have on moral consciousness without misrepresenting them in the manner of Habermasian self-reflection. It introduces an attitude of suspicion without claiming special insight or competence, and without removing its perceptions from dialogue.

The practice of criticism thus both opposes and appropriates traditional practice. As situated reflection, it operates against a background of evaluations, while as an exercise in suspicion it unveils what stands behind habitual signification. Critique seeks liberation from the dogmatism of conventional speech, and thus avoids falling back into an unreflective endorsement of existing conditions. However, as noted in my discussion of Foucault, opposition is invariably parasitic on affirmation. Even the demystification of genealogical analysis and ideology critique depends for its intelligibility on a prior valorization. We criticize moral action not by pointing to an inherent evil, but by showing how the action betrays a principle or violates what we deem important. Negation and advocacy exist in a dialectical relationship. To negate is already to have affirmed, and to affirm is to be capable of negation. We can thus say with Gadamer (and against Habermas) that "reflection is not always and unavoidably a step towards dissolving prior convictions."[24] Bringing something to awareness may lead toward either acceptance or rejection, including those evaluations that are passed down through tradition.

There is no need for a critical hermeneutics to follow Habermas in invoking Freud's distinction between manifest and latent meaning. While suspicious interpretation is a disclosure of what present understanding conceals, this ought not to be inflated into the quasi-scientific view that critique is a movement from manifest to latent meaning. Hermeneutics rejects the possibility of a science of meaning on the premise that text analogues are invariably underdetermined, potentially taking on new meaning in the course of interpretation. To speak of criticism as decipherment is not to rehabilitate essentialist talk of objective meaning, but to reconceive the relation between concealment and disclosure. Rather than speaking of interpretation as "seeing through" a manifest meaning to an underlying latency, it is more appropriate to conceive of interpretation as at once concealment and unconcealment, as *lethe* and *aletheia*. Meaning is never a total disclosure but a perspectival and necessarily incomplete description. This is to say with Heidegger that "concealment, *lethe*, belongs to *a-letheia*, not just as an addition, not as shadow to light, but rather as the heart of *aletheia*."[25] Viewing concealment and disclosure as dialectically correlative enables us to speak of interpretation as "unmasking" without making metaphysical distinctions between objective and subjective, latent and manifest, meaning.

That the dialectic of concealment and disclosure arises not only in textual exegesis but in social criticism may be seen in the following example. Egalitarian discourse in its several forms brings to light hitherto undetected relations of power, subtle oppressions and treacheries of various kinds. It modifies the terms of moral debate by accentuating elements of our practices that had either escaped notice or had been regarded as inconsequential. Yet at the same time, egalitarian criticism frequently gives rise to new forms of mystification. It conceals and thereby legitimizes new forms of hegemony. This includes everything from violations of liberty to cultural leveling to other expressions of the will to power. One need only recall the history of Christian morality or Marxist politics to see how egalitarian narrative, in attuning reflection toward specific ills and inequalities, introduces and conceals new ills and inequalities.

Criticism invites us to change our perceptions without attaining the rigor of foundational or scientific knowledge. Because the meaning of a text analogue is inexhaustible, interpretation leads not to a final determination or telling blow but to a perpetual retelling, a dialogue in which no interpretation constitutes the definitive truth. Further, since imagination is shared by all language users, no person may claim expert status in social criticism. No matter how illuminating our perceptions, there is no conveying of privilege on grounds of special competence or superior moral development, but only the continuing to-and-fro of debate. The practice of criticism is profoundly misconceived as an expertocratic bestowing of "enlightenment" upon ideologically duped masses. The asymmetrical relationship between therapist and patient in psychoanalysis, or between scientist and research subject in the Kohlbergian moral judgment interview, is not transferable to social criticism.

Hermeneutics undermines neither the emancipatory intent of criticism nor its capacity to question traditional practice. Without fashioning superinterpretations explaining the "real" factors operative behind the facade of language and tradition, criticism brings to light what is concealed by present understanding. It includes a moment of recollection and of semantic innovation, and involves the incessant reinterpretation of the language in which a culture understands itself and its practices. It transforms what is given into what is questionable and reveals new dimensions of meaning, recognizing that its perceptions also conceal. Critique is the deconstruction and reconstruction of social reality by means of moral imagination. It also serves an iconoclastic function, reminding us of the contingency and partiality of our perceptions. As an exercise in suspicion, it undermines the dogmatic certainty of traditional belief while maintaining the capacity for affirmation. While we may think of reflection generally as a bringing to awareness, critical reflection specifically is a bringing to awareness in order to provoke a current mode of seeing-as. It places interpretations at risk, suspending their validity by confronting them with alternative descriptions. To understand critically is not only to "see as," but to see as this rather than that. Critique is thus inseparable not only from imagination but from dialogue, since contestation occurs through conversation with persons occupying different perspectives.

Since everything that can be described can be redescribed, there is in principle nothing preventing every morally interesting action or institution from becoming an object of criticism. While reflection occurs from a finite perspective, we are always capable of using semantic innovation to extend the limits of our ethical/political horizon. The language of social criticism remains open to imaginative usage and tolerates the introduction of new metaphorical and narrative constructions. Only the possibility of assessing all norms and practices simultaneously or from a privileged standpoint is lost by the failure of totalizing reflection.

Application and Practical Judgment

Social criticism's moment of affirmation is informed not only by values appropriated from tradition but by principles theoretically articulated. Applying principles to cases is often regarded as a procedure of formal derivation. Principles, conceived as decision procedures formulated in advance of particular cases, function as major premises in a practical syllogism. Formalists abstract a single dominant consideration from a given case — whether the act in question maximizes utility, passes the test of universalizability, and so on. In each instance, rational choice is a matter of applying the particular case to ready-made principles and deriving judgments in rule-governed fashion, eliminating any significant reliance on the personal responsibility of the judging subject. Practical reasoning is thus assimilated to mathematical and scientific models of derivation and quantitative calculus.

The formalist policy of abstracting from the contingencies of a case and applying rules in deductive fashion has met with the charge of context insensitivity. Its preoccupation with a single moral consideration and exclusion of potentially overriding factors fails to do justice to the individual case. An excessive preoccupation with rules may prevent one from qualifying a judgment or rendering an exception in light of extenuating circumstances, or of modifying the rule itself due to unforeseen conditions to which a rule may fail to do justice. Critics of ethical formalism oppose the rigidity of its procedures and favor less simplistic models of practical reasoning. Aristotelians in particular caution against the expectation of scientific or mathematical rigor, urging us to refrain from glossing over the complexities of particular contexts and to adopt a more responsive attitude toward particulars. Justice requires that attention be directed equally toward universals and particulars in all their complexity.

Practical reasoning in both the Aristotelian and hermeneutical traditions (particularly as represented in Gadamer's thought) is not a formal method of derivation, but an interpretive art. It involves hermeneutic perception of a context in light of normative principles. Rather than viewing the application of principles as an operation governed by algorithms, hermeneutics regards application as itself a part of the interpretive process. We understand the case by identifying the principle of which it is an instance.

Following Aristotle, Gadamer distinguishes between knowledge in the applied sciences and in the application of normative principles. The former, governed by a technological understanding of the theory/practice relation, apply clear, distinct principles known in advance. A proper application of principles subsumes the case at hand according to general theoretical requirements. Ideally (if counterfactually), technological practice constitutes a perfect instantiation of scientific principles while the relation between the two is one of strict subordination.[26] By contrast, hermeneutics regards the practice of applying principles as fundamentally unlike the technical application of the applied sciences. Normative principles are neither grasped clearly and distinctly nor fully determined apart from the contexts in which they are instantiated. While determining what morality requires in a given case involves an application of principles, such application does not involve standing over against the case and affixing to it a principle that could be fully comprehended in abstract form. It is better regarded as a reading of the situation — a perception of its moral significance — from within the situation itself. As an interpreter, one is not an observer of something standing over against one, but is caught up in an effort to understand the case in light of a principle. It is as an instantiation of a universal that the particular is understood, a universal not fully determined apart from its applications.

This view is represented in Gadamer's assertion that the practice of understanding is inextricably bound up not only with interpretation but with application. Principles are never entirely understood abstracted from their practical applications, just as understanding the meaning of a text involves applying the text to the reader's own situation. As Gadamer writes, application "can never signify a subsidiary operation appended as an afterthought to understanding: the object of our application determines from the beginning and in its totality the real and concrete content of hermeneutical understanding. Application is not a calibration of some generality given in advance in order to unravel afterwards a particular situation. In attending to a text, for example, the interpreter does not try to apply a general criterion to a particular case; on the contrary, he is interested in the fundamentally original significance of the writing under his consideration." It is mistaken to regard application as a practice in which a determinate particular is subsumed under an equally determinate universal. Universals only come into being in the process of being instantiated in, or applied to, particular contexts.

This is the meaning of Gadamer's thesis that understanding and application (as well as interpretation) must be regarded "as comprising one unified process."[27]

To illustrate this, let us briefly consider the case of human rights. While it is possible to define approximately what these principles mean, such definitions underdetermine the meaning of rights. They lack content until we understand their significance in concrete terms, the forms of legislation in which they have their being. The conventional understanding of rights as universal standards must be qualified by pointing out that the critical distance such principles make possible is never complete since the principles that inform criticism must themselves be understood, in significant measure, in light of their applications. To understand a given principle, one must know its sphere of application and the conflicts that it resolves. The principle of democracy may be defined as rule by the people, for the people, and of the people, but this definition is unmistakeably and inescapably vague. We understand democracy in the realm of political practice.

Aristotle held that practical moral knowledge (*phronesis*) involves a reciprocity between universal and particular which is entirely absent in technical and scientific knowledge (*techne, episteme*), and which is not governed by formal methods. Unlike technical knowledge, which begins with a clear and distinct grasp of both the ends it sets out to achieve and the methods of achieving them, and which applies its principles in a more or less automatic way, *phronesis* is responsive to the contingencies of particular situations and involves a reciprocal illumination of general principles and particular cases. In *phronesis*, universal and particular co-determine each other. The perception of the particular case is mediated by a principle of which the particular is seen as an instance. The principle, in other words, educates perception by illuminating the morally salient features of a given case. Principles are also mediated by particulars since the latter give concrete determination and content to the former.

Another point of distinction between application in ethics and in the applied sciences concerns the absence of rules governing the former. Unlike technical modes of thought, the application of normative principles is not governed by algorithms. There are no second order principles for determining the correct implementation of first order principles. The reason for this is twofold. First, an infinite regress arises whenever we seek a methodological basis for the application of moral principles.[28] If the application of first order principles were directed by second order principles, their application would require the guidance of third order principles, and so on *ad infinitum*. Second, judgment that is properly responsive to particularities — which does not subsume particulars dogmatically but examines each case on its merits — is far too complex to be captured within a set of rules. It is, for instance, characteristic of principles to permit exceptions, many of which cannot be catalogued in advance. The formalist view would need either to forbid exceptions (thus opening itself to the charge of rule fetishism) or to provide further rules determining which types of cases are to be treated as exceptions, as well as a rule for deciding on the proper course once a special case is recognized. The difficulty in formulating rules of this kind is that special cases are anomalous and perhaps unrepeatable. While there may be certain classes of exceptions that can be anticipated in advance, most must be treated on a case-by-case basis.

The most complex algorithms cannot map the prudent application of principles. Application is properly regarded as a practical skill in bringing universals and particulars to bear on each other without following rules. It is a capacity for mediating between principles and cases, a capacity that requires hermeneutic perceptiveness rather than formal derivations. Practical reasoning may illuminate a case by likening it to a similar case encountered in the past (a precedent). It proceeds not only from universal to particular, and vice versa, but also from particular to relevantly similar particular (without rules for deciding what constitutes a relevant similarity). The function of the universal here is to link distinct but related instances, to render both intelligible without overlooking their particularity. Thus, practical reasoning illuminates universals and particulars not methodologically but analogically.

Much of the difficulty of normative criticism lies in its nonalgorithmic application of principles, its subsumption of a particular under an appropriate universal without criteria of appropriateness. Moral disagreement is sometimes interminable, even among speakers upholding identical principles, because we are without rules for determining how principles ought to be applied and must rely on the judgment of individuals. *Phronesis* or practical judgment must be employed in resolving these kinds of difficulties. Because there are no rules governing the subsumption of particulars, it is *phronesis* that determines which principle is brought to bear upon the case at hand. One must decide what kind of issue it is and which principle is appropriate in resolving it — a matter often far from self-evident. The difficulty is compounded when more than one principle may be brought to bear, and when they generate conflicting judgments; then one must decide which principle takes priority and why. Nor are there rules determining a course of action once the appropriate principle is identified. We may still disagree about how the principle would best be applied given all the facts of the case.

Practical judgment is also required in situations where we must decide whether a given case qualifies as an exception to a principle. We must decide, again without rules, whether extenuating circumstances are sufficient to justify granting an exception or tempering judgment. Judgment is also called for when traditional norms are unable to cope with new realities and must be modified or replaced.[29] Practical judgment is then required in refashioning the rules themselves.

Aristotelians and other nonformalists who accentuate the role of *phronesis* in practical reasoning are often charged with vagueness by schools of thought that insist on formal methods of adjudication and application. A measure of ambiguity, however, seems an ineluctable feature of moral reasoning. A fully explicit theory of judgment specifying precisely how it functions or ought to function should not be expected. "[P]recision is not to be sought for alike in all discussions," Aristotle reminds us.[30] Practical judgment is a skill for mediating between universal and particular without following rules. It is a capacity for interpreting and reasoning about particular contexts which, while employing principles, is not governed by them, nor by formal methods or criteria. It is a skill in detecting the salient features of moral action and in subsuming particulars under the appropriate principle. With Kant, we may say that "judgment in general is the faculty of thinking the particular as contained under the universal," whether the universal is a concept, rule, principle, or law.[31] Practical judgment is judgment when neither universal nor particular is immediately given. It is neither "reflective" nor "determinant" in Kant's sense: it is neither the case that the particular is given and we have to find the appropriate universal under which to subsume it, nor that the universal is given and we must determine which particular belongs under it. The principle illuminates the object of reflection and the object of reflection simultaneously illuminates (or determines the content of) the principle. The being of both universal and particular are determined dialectically in the act of judging.

As a skill,[32] practical judgment does not generate conclusions deductively but aims at reconciling a principle with a given case in a way that is "fitting" or "suitable." The vagueness of these expressions is unavoidable since there are no necessary and sufficient conditions determining their abstract content. Nor is there a substantive common feature uniting all instances (possible or actual) of good judgment. While what is suitable in many instances is a more or less straightforward application of a principle, good judgment is a matter of flexibly tailoring a principle to the complexity of a given case. Establishing a just fit between universal and particular is not determined by rules but is the nature of skillful activity. The skillful performance of an action or art includes a practical knowledge of how to tailor general requirements to the complexities of particular situations without consulting rules. Indeed, a primary point of distinction between one who has mastered a skill and a novice is that the former is not forever consulting rules but has an intuitive sense based on training and experience of how to execute a certain range of tasks.[33]

As a skill, practical judgment depends on the perceptiveness and responsibility of the individual judge. It is not demonstrative knowledge or privileged insight into deep moral truths, yet neither is it merely a feeling or an arbitrary act of decision. Practical judgment is a reflective act of reasoning which is able to see what is required and respond appropriately. While falling outside the province of deduction and induction, it is capable of providing a reasoned defense of its evaluations. In practical reasoning one is not relieved of the responsibility of justifying one's evaluations, but one's justification does not compel agreement or constitute proof. The reasons to which it points are not constituted from a general rule but from particular features of a case. One might, for instance, defend one's characterization of an act as courageous by drawing attention to obstacles the agent had to overcome in performing it. The claim that individual freedom has been violated might be justified by pointing out the specific manner in which the person's options have been restricted by the will of another. Practical reasoning is concerned with particulars, and it is the particular features of an action or context that are appealed to in efforts at justification.[34]

Practical judgment involves the capacity to identify the salient features of a case in light of our experience and training as moral agents. The moral education and character of the individual invariably inform the capacity to reason about the fit between principles and their applications. As Aristotle maintained, practical judgment is not only the ability to reason well but an intellectual virtue inseparable from the ethical virtues. It is acquired together with the latter virtues in the process of moral education.

Practical judgment also includes an important element of sociality. It is informed not only by the training and experience of the individual but by the collective experience of a community, drawing on implicit understandings of ourselves and of the traditions and communities of which we are a part. Within the collective conversations of a community moral perceptions are modified and refined, becoming less idiosyncratic and increasingly intersubjective. The locus of practical reason thus shifts from the judgment and training of the individual speaker to the wider social practice of hermeneutic dialogue, the social or intersubjective counterpart of *phronesis*. Practical judgment is thus ultimately inseparable from the practice of ordinary hermeneutic dialogue.

These notions of hermeneutic application and judgment are clearly located within the tradition of practical philosophy stemming from the *Nicomachean Ethics* and extending into philosophical hermeneutics. The dialectical conception of principles and their applications represents a particular instance of the more general doctrine of the hermeneutic circle,[35] and is thus firmly situated within the hermeneutical tradition. Practical reasoning, however, also has an important heritage within American pragmatism, particularly as represented in the thought of John Dewey. For hermeneuticists and pragmatists alike, the relation between principles and individual cases is one of reciprocity or two-way illumination. Both oppose the traditional polarization of theory and practice and the subordination of the latter to the former. Here emerges an important convergence between the two schools of thought.[36]

In the pragmatic tradition, theory is not an end in itself but a means of remedying social ills and facilitating our commerce with the world. The rationality of theories and principles is determined not solely on the basis of their conceptual rigor but by their power to enhance human practices. In particular, Dewey's pragmatic ethics seeks not to "ground" social practices but to critique and enhance them. Ethical theorizing is redeemed only through its practical applications. Dewey's pragmatic conception of the value and function of normative theory demonstrates an orientation toward the identification of specific social ills and away from abstract generalities and decision procedures. Principles are applied to cases in an experimental fashion and always with an eye to their consequences. The pragmatic emphasis on consequences — not merely the "logical entailments" of principles but their actual effects on persons and practices — gives rise to a mode of reasoning that Dewey terms "experimental intelligence." Practical reasoning is likened to experimentation in that it proceeds by anticipating the consequences of a principle's application, following its progress through various steps, and arriving at a determination informed by the consequences. Judgments are held in the tentative manner of hypotheses until the effects brought about by the application of a principle are known.

Both particular judgments and general principles must be tested and revised in light of their practical consequences. Principles, for Dewey, are not followed to the letter like bureaucratic regulations or categorical imperatives, but are hypotheses in the sense that they are applied as means of serving practical ends. For Dewey, the "principles which man projects as guides of reconstructive action, are not dogmas. They are hypotheses to be worked out in practice, and to be rejected, corrected and expanded as they fail or succeed in giving our present experience the guidance it requires. We may call them programmes of action, but since they are to be used in making our future acts less blind, more directed, they are flexible. Intelligence is not something possessed once for all. It is in constant process of forming, and its retention requires constant alertness in observing consequences, an open-minded will to learn and courage in re-adjustment."[37] Herein lies an important distinction Dewey draws between principles and rules. Whereas the latter are fixed procedures for the direction of specific courses of action and are applicable in all cases regardless of the outcomes produced, principles serve more modestly to provide a basis for the analysis of moral contexts by directing attention toward their salient features. Principles are modified to suit particular cases in a manner reminiscent of Aristotelian *phronesis*.[38] Pragmatic application is attentive to complexity and to the myriad of effects that may follow upon a principle's implementation. It is such effects, rather than adherence to a rule, that are ultimately authoritative in determining a principle's appropriateness in a given case. To apply a principle is thus always to apply it differently since application requires a creative effort at interpreting both the case at hand and the principle brought to bear on it. Prudent application constitutes the antithesis of the straightforward repetition of prior determinations. Principles rigidly upheld without regard for the consequences of their application are not principles in the pragmatic sense but fixed and dogmatic rules.

The pragmatic notion of application thus demonstrates an affinity with Aristotle's notion of equity (*epieikeia*), the intellectual virtue described in the *Nicomachean Ethics* as the "correction of legal justice."[39] Principles and laws formulated in general terms are not without a certain deficiency in matters of application. They are articulated in abstraction from cases while moral actions are necessarily particular. The generality of principles never catches up with the particularity of human action. Human action contains complexities that principles formulated in abstract terms cannot anticipate, thus requiring flexibility in adapting principles to individual cases. "For when the thing is indefinite," Aristotle writes, "the rule also is indefinite, like the leaden rule used in making the Lesbian moulding; the rule adapts itself to the shape of the stone and is not rigid" (1137b29–30). For Aristotelians and pragmatists alike, it is flexibility and not pedantry that is the mark of practical reasonableness.

Dewey reserves some of his harshest criticism for philosophers who so privilege theoretical concepts, rules, and decision procedures that they become oblivious to the practical consequences of moral reasoning.[40] This attitude is perhaps best represented by the Kantian moralist, whose a priori laws and unconditional duties excessively narrow the field of moral investigation and give rise to rigidity in disposition and judgment. This very unpragmatic turn of mind gives aid and comfort to the moral absolutist who makes conformity to rules a virtue unto itself. Rule fetishism makes a virtue of servility and confuses conscientious action with an unimaginative adherence to rules, as if these were a kind of transcendental deliverance. In the quest for moral certainty, some become mesmerized by the theoretical elegance and logical precision of our principles and lose sight of what principles are for: critiquing social practices, resolving conflicts, and fostering efforts at mutual accommodation. Like dead metaphors, principles deteriorate into idols when their connection with practice is lost sight of.

Normative concepts include a measure of indeterminacy which precludes exhaustive analysis of their content. Their meaning, as Gadamer notes, is "not fixed in the firmament like the stars; they are what they are only in the concrete situations in which we find ourselves."[41] A principle is the history (the "effective history," as Gadamer would say) of its applications, its meaning being supplemented on each occasion of its implementation, just as the meaning of a text is disclosed anew in each instance of its interpretation. Principles lack both precise boundaries and a precisely specifiable common property which would make each of its applications a true instance of the principle. The applications of a principle contain only what Wittgenstein calls family resemblances: they "have no one thing in common which makes us use the same word for all, — but . . . they are *related* to one another in many different ways."[42] It is on account of displaying any one of several related qualities — and not a single essential property — that we characterize a particular case as an application of a principle, while the principle itself is merely this set of overlapping resemblances. The principle is understood analogically and not *sub specie aeternitatus.*

Being hermeneutic in structure, normative principles are subject to interpretation even while informing interpretation. There is a double indeterminacy here: human action, being without a fully determinate meaning, is understood through interpretation and judged in the light of a principle which itself lacks a univocal meaning and is interpreted anew in each case of its application. The meaning of both the principle and the situation on which it sheds light are underdetermined on their own, and are codetermined in practical reasoning. While there is an inevitable degree of indeterminacy here, indeterminacy should not be construed as arbitrariness. It would be best to renounce such dichotomies — still operative within numerous schools of moral and political philosophy — as reason and decision, knowledge and opinion, theory and practice. Dichotomies of this kind had their credentials established by moral epistemologies that promised metaphysical foundations and transcendental guarantees, and these epistemologies can no longer be taken seriously. They presuppose, among other untenable premises, the availability of unassailable decision procedures, that principles are known clearly and distinctly, and that human conduct has a single determinate meaning. The fallibility of practical judgment — the possibility that our evaluations may need to be reexamined on occasion, that our principles may require periodic revision, or that we may be in error — is not a formula for irrationalism, but a reminder of the conditions and limits of reflection.

Five

Hermeneutical Ethical Theory

Recent nonfoundationalist challenges raise the issue of whether the task of theory construction in moral and political philosophy is still a useful one or whether such a project is untenable and superfluous. The question arises whether a hermeneutical ethics leaves us merely with the injunction to continue "the conversation that we are," to fashion perpetually novel metaphorical and narrative constructions in unending dialogue without offering normative principles to inform the practice of criticism. Opponents of normative theory regard the project of justifying universal principles as being as doomed to failure as the foundationalist project in epistemology, raising the question whether hermeneutical ethics must join the ranks of antitheory or whether a theory can be fashioned that would inform social criticism while satisfying objections to traditional theories.

Acknowledging the embeddedness of hermeneutic reflection does not preclude the possibility of fashioning a universalist concept of justice; indeed, such a conception is indispensable in articulating a critique of power. Defending this view challenges dichotomies — an ethics of principles or an ethics of judgment, universality or historicity, objectivism or relativism, sameness or alterity — that have emerged in much recent nonfoundationalist literature. Abandoning totalizing perspectives precludes only certain forms of normative theorizing, including attempts both to privilege a particular conception of the good or to eliminate the need for practical judgment through formal decision procedures. The task of normative theory is not to prescribe particular courses of action or to provide a grounding for social practices, but to inform critical reflection by articulating principles of universal right, principles that inform while constraining interpretation. These principles do not provide an exhaustive analysis of the moral domain, rendering local norms and capacities of perception morally irrelevant.

An historically conscious universalist concept of justice, which takes its bearings from the liberal tradition while incorporating premises from Gadamer's hermeneutics and Habermas's communicative ethics, furnishes critical reflection with a principled framework in which the freedom and equality of persons may be recognized. Hermeneutical ethical theory places constraints on local norms, institutions, and practices of power by rendering explicit the normative dimension inherent in the practice of communicative understanding.

The Primacy of Practice and the Case Against Theory

The principal aim of modern normative theories has been to identify universal principles that justify particular judgments and practices. Principles provide the theorist with decision procedures for resolving problems generated by conflicting norms and preferences. Philosophers have applied principles to ground social practices and provide a theoretical blueprint of ethical relations. The traditional epistemology-centered conception of philosophy held that the task of theory construction was to provide a rational grounding for normative appraisal, rendering judgments invulnerable to the arguments of the moral skeptic.

In recent decades, this view has been called into question by several nonfoundationalist schools of thought. Opponents of theory argue that once we dispense with foundationalist epistemology we shall no longer feel compelled to ground normative judgments on something that transcends social practices. They contend that the search for a philosophical basis of our moral lives ought to be abandoned along with the foundationalist quest for certainty in epistemology, suspecting that we are unlikely to uncover a common source of moral standards or gain a universal theoretical perspective on local norms. This suspicion arises not only from the decline of foundationalist epistemology but from a rising skepticism about a metaphysics of human nature or the moral law, traditional candidates for the role of foundation of ethical life. Antitheorists argue that evaluations are not in need of constraints beyond local consensus, and that the primacy of theoretical reason over local practices ought to be reversed. Moral argument need appeal to nothing more than the historically contingent behavioral and discursive practices that take hold in a lifeworld. Already reflective, such practices do not require theoretical grounding.

As we have seen, opposition to normative theorizing is a prominent theme in the writings of Foucault. While his genealogical writings contain an unmistakeable ethical-political dimension, Foucault refrains from adopting a universal or theoretical standpoint in his historical investigations, instead viewing criticism as occurring from the perspective of specific practices and institutions without the assistance of a theoretical framework. Foucault rules out unifying perspectives because of the philosophical impossibility of taking up an external position with respect to modern practices and because the fascination with theoretical unity hinders attempts to gain a concrete understanding of power relations. While theories like Marxism and psychoanalysis may help carry out specific investigations, Foucault cautions against their overextension. Their unifying capacity must not be exaggerated in a manner that would reintroduce totalizing perspectives for social criticism. Foucault's "specific intellectual" analyzes social phenomena from a participatory standpoint, attending always to the concrete workings of various practices and institutions without ever attaining the distanced perspective of the universal intellectual.

A similar stance is taken by Jean-François Lyotard, who formulates his conception of justice largely as a response to certain themes of political modernity. Lyotard replaces consensus, universality, finality, and other touchstones of modern political thought with divergence, contestation, novelty, and opinion. Political discourse aims not at convergence but at a perpetual invention of novel utterances. Justice belongs to the order of opinion and not to the order of knowledge or truth. "There is," Lyotard writes, "no knowledge in matters of ethics. And therefore there will be no knowledge in matters of politics."[1] Following the sophists in this regard, Lyotard also follows Aristotle in asserting the priority of practical judgment over method and theoretical frameworks. In political and ethical matters, he argues, judgments are fashioned without the aid of criteria of any kind. They are neither regulated by criteria, nor educated by training and habit, nor guided by common sense, but are instead essentially decisionistic. "One is without criteria, yet one must decide" (17). All talk of criteria in postmodernity, Lyotard supposes, is illegitimate since "the idea of criteria comes from the discourse of truth and supposes a referent or a 'reality' and, by dint of this, it does not belong to the discourse of justice. This is very important. It must be understood that if one wants criteria in the discourse of justice one is tolerating de facto the encroachment of the discourse of justice by the discourse of truth" (98).

We are faced on Lyotard's account with two antithetical conceptions of normative discourse. We may seek a science of politics — grounding evaluative judgments in theoretical statements pertaining either to the nature of reason, human nature, natural law, or something of the kind — or we may form judgments on a case-by-case basis without principles or criteria of any kind. Preferring the latter,

Lyotard contends that a politics of judgment must forswear all theoretical "metanarratives" and reinstate the rights of small and local narratives. The role of the philosopher is to hazard opinions and submit judgments to the general discussion and not to devise theories concerning the nature of justice.

Perhaps the most noted opponent of normative theory on this side of the Atlantic is Richard Rorty, who urges us to give up all talk of philosophical foundations and of grounding practices and commitments in anything transcending those practices and commitments. It is no more necessary (or possible) to detach ourselves from such commitments by theoretical means than it is to step outside of our language to verify its resemblance to objective states of affairs. The values available to social criticism are in no sense axiomatic but are "never more than the platitudes which contextually define the terms of a final vocabulary currently in use."[2] The only constraints on moral action, as well as on what passes for the truth, are consensual ones. They are not universal principles deduced from metaphysical assumptions but historically contingent commitments that have managed to generate consensus within a particular culture at a particular time.

The thesis defended by these and other opponents of normative theory concerning the primacy of practice — the thesis that social practices are sufficiently reflective as not to require the kind of grounding that foundationalist theories sought to provide — is by now a familiar one in nonfoundationalist, hermeneutical, and postmodern circles. The foundationalist project has been ably deconstructed, but assenting to the view that normative rationality takes its bearings from the realm of practice does not entail abandoning normative theory in all its forms. Time and again it is intimated that we must choose between a theoretical grounding of ethical life or socialized decisionism, a priori principles of reason or a final vocabulary, knowledge or opinion, and so on. In each instance, we are urged to abandon the former for the latter, a move usually accompanied by an expression of skepticism or exasperation with the first alternative. Those of us inclined to share Nietzsche's distrust of dichotomies would sooner challenge the dichotomies themselves than abandon one pole for the other, a move that normally creates as many problems as it solves.

The problems generated by renouncing theory for practice, principles for judgment, and so on, emerge in the transition from skeptical argument about the possibility of objective grounds (argument that is frequently compelling) to the stage of the argument in which a specific normative standpoint is defended. If critical reflection has the dialectical structure spoken of in chapter four — if it has the capacity both to negate and to affirm — it is the latter, affirmative, moment of reflection that is often a source of difficulty for opponents of normative theory.

Foucault, Lyotard, Rorty, and other contemporary antitheorists suggest that we must remain on the lookout for relations of power, forced consensus, and bad metaphysics and that we must reinstate subjugated knowledges, defend the rights of local narratives, celebrate plurality, and so on. Thus without offering a detailed ethical or political program, their writing has an unmistakeable normative thrust and a similarity of themes and moral passions.[3] The moral horizon that they occupy broadly affirms the virtues of (left-) liberal democracy, with relatively minor differences separating them. The sentiments expressed in the following passages from Rorty and Lyotard respectively are representative of this partial convergence of moral and political commitments.

> I want to see freely arrived at agreement as agreement on how to accomplish common purposes (e.g., prediction and control of the behavior of atoms or people, equalizing life-chances, decreasing cruelty), but I want to see these common purposes against the background of an increasing sense of the radical diversity of private purposes, of the radically poetic character of individual lives, and of the merely poetic foundations of the 'we-consciousness' which lies behind our social institutions.[4]

> And the idea that I think we need today in order to make decisions
> in political matters cannot be the idea of the totality, or of the unity,
> of a body. It can only be the idea of a multiplicity or of a diversity.[5]

Difficulties arise when we inevitably inquire into the philosophical rationale of this particular constellation of values. Abandoning
the foundationalist quest does not relieve philosophers of the responsibility of providing an account of their ethical-political commitments. If we accept the inescapability of the dichotomies
mentioned above, the only reply, offered by Rorty, is that we must
not allow the epistemologist's or skeptic's "why" questions to become a cause for anxiety, tempting us thereby into making a
foundationalist move of one kind or another. We should admit that
"we are just the historical moment that we are,"[6] that justification
need appeal to nothing beyond the sphere of local norms, practices, and institutions that define our way of life. This response
would have to suffice were the only alternative the kind of objective grounding sought by conventional normative theories.

Does the "lonely provincialism"[7] of a Rorty or a Lyotard have
sufficient resources to inform social criticism concerning both the
practices of our own culture and those of foreign cultures? How
are we to justify philosophically the moral and political commitments that we make? Justifying them by appealing to local solidarities carries a degree of force in that such appeals succeed in bringing
together our evaluations with our mode of self-understanding.
Human beings do not form evaluative judgments in isolation from
an understanding of who they are, what their history is, and what
they would like to become. Questions of the good, for instance, are
frequently answered in light of who we understand ourselves to be
and how we narrate our history. However, in matters of justice,
appeals to local solidarity encounter difficulties. It is not uncom-
mon for norms to ossify or become corrupted. Communities and
their often self-appointed representatives are not immune from
dogmatism. Once they decide that they are in possession of the
truth, it is not only religious communities and authoritarian states

that are liable to ominous forms of intolerance. Communities may (and frequently do) become so enamored with what comes to pass for truth within their borders or on their membership lists that their concern for justice takes a back seat to an agenda, clinging to an outmoded belief system, or retaining power.

As any number of historical examples illustrate, basing moral claims on local consensus can lead to a crude majoritarianism or a recipe for intolerance. Settled convictions must be occasionally unsettled, yet attempts to question such convictions are negated by unreflective appeals to "community standards" or "the American way." While even very unreflective communities are capable of critical reflection, the limits of reflection become a cause for concern when a community's judgments and the standards used in adjudicating them deteriorate or are dubious from the start. When the self-understanding that underlies a community's norms is infected with bad metaphysical schemes, dubious religious beliefs, and abhorrent attitudes, the difficulty in assessing such norms is especially pronounced.

Difficulties also occur when an object of criticism is distant in time or place. Rorty insists that there can be no noncircular justification of a final vocabulary. The adoption of a vocabulary is a matter of social decision, not philosophical argumentation. At most, we can defend our settled convictions by showing how they favorably compare with those of foreign cultures. A pragmatic justification takes the form of intersocietal comparisons in which one demonstrates the practical advantages of our own norms and institutions over various alternatives.[8] The problem lies in the degree of force social criticism that is "by our lights" can claim when it takes foreign institutions and norms as its object. When we take exception, for instance, to the treatment in certain cultures of "infidels", "heretics," "untouchables," or "counterrevolutionaries" by pointing out how such treatment violates norms that we in our tradition consider important, it is unclear why anyone who stands outside of our tradition should regard this as a forceful criticism — or indeed as a criticism at all, as opposed to an announcement that we happen to hold a different view. Absent from such a critique is a reason why anyone who does not share our final vocabulary ought to share our moral attitudes.

A further problem in criticizing even the most abhorrent practices of foreign cultures is that often such practices are readily justifiable in the final vocabulary of that culture. For every inquisition or religious crusade there is an ancient tradition of belief, a moral vocabulary, popular norms, and established institutions. That theocratic or totalitarian states often persist for as long as they do testifies to the self-legitimating character of final vocabularies. As local solidarities legitimate themselves, so they legitimate what become difficult to recognize as oppressive institutions.

Rorty argues that we may lend support to our final vocabulary by showing how it favorably compares with others in terms of practical advantages. Yet this overlooks that what is regarded as advantageous is itself far from vocabulary-neutral. The notion of an advantage is intelligible only in light of a set of prior values; it is a function of the final vocabulary one has adopted, just as the good is a reflection of a prior self-understanding. If, as a consequence of the tradition one inherits, one regards as advantageous preserving the party's grip on power, enlightening the infidel, or creating the divine kingdom on earth, then Rorty's intersocietal comparisons will merely confirm one's prejudices. The circularity of pragmatic justification and ethnocentric appeals, in short, attenuates social criticism by offering no reason for those who do not share the critic's vocabulary and think as the critic does to reform their institutions.

Contributions from hermeneutical philosophers to this debate take as their point of departure a set of premises largely similar to that of Rorty, Lyotard, and Foucault, while taking up positions distinct, in varying degrees, from all three.[9] Without renouncing normative theory, these authors are inclined to accentuate the situated and practical character of moral reasoning. Taking Gadamer's hermeneutics as their primary inspiration, P. Christopher Smith,

Matthew Foster, and Georgia Warnke attempt to draw out the normative implications of Gadamer's thought.[10] (Gadamer himself, while clearly interested in ethical questions, has not articulated an ethical or political theory, nor defended any particular political program.) With Foucault, Lyotard, and Rorty, these authors oppose normative theory that seeks grounds external to local practices and traditions upon which to base an objective assessment. Principles are not generated by autonomous reason but inherited from tradition. As Smith expresses it, "our sense of what is right and wrong, good and bad, fair and disgraceful, is transmitted to us in the language we have inherited, and that language, sustained as it is by the inexplicit customs we are accustomed to, capacitates us to deliberate well and make ethical choices."[11] The task of a hermeneutical ethical theory, in their view, is not to provide a foundation for evaluative judgments but to recover principles from tradition and to clarify the meaning of local norms. Its task, in Warnke's words, is "to uncover and articulate the principles already embedded in or implied by a community's practices, institutions and norms of action. The theory of justice becomes an attempt to understand what a society's actions, practices and norms mean, to elucidate for a culture what its shared understandings are so that it can agree on the principles of justice that make sense to it and for it."[12] The theorist is an interpreter of cultural norms and tradition rather than their transcendental judge, contesting their significance through conflicting, and often equally compelling, interpretations.

Hermeneutical conceptions of ethics focus not on justifying abstract and universal principles but on the practice of dialogue and its promotion in matters of public policy. Because ethical theorizing is concerned with the interpretation of local practices and traditions and provides no philosophical methods of adjudicating conflicting understandings of social meaning, we are left with a kind of hermeneutic pluralism. Debate over the suitability of norms and institutions never culminates in anything beyond a provisional consensus. Nor is such consensus a guaranteed outcome of communicative

exchanges. Frequently, the result of hermeneutic dialogue is a recognition that there are legitimate differences of opinion, with no
procedure for deciding which view ought to command assent.

In lieu of such procedures, moral theorists must remain open to
the possibility of learning from opposed viewpoints, just as traditions may gain something of value in encountering other traditions.
Without having recourse to universal principles, a tradition may
test itself against other traditions in much the way that interpretations may be tested against other interpretations without recourse
to methodological criteria. So conceived, the justification of customs and evaluations is a matter of hermeneutic dialogue. While
such conversation may or may not generate consensus on the meaning or relative importance of a given norm, it is within this practice
that the one-sidedness of interpretation is overcome. As Warnke
expresses it, hermeneutical ethics gives rise to an interpretive pluralism and to democratic decision-making.

> The idea behind the notion of hermeneutic conversation is the idea
> that an interpretive pluralism can be educational for all the parties
> involved. If we are to be educated by interpretations other than our
> own, however, we must both encourage the articulation of those
> alternative interpretations and help to make them as compelling as
> they can be. And how can we do this except by assuring the fairness
> of the conversation and working to give all possible voices equal
> access? If we are to learn from our hermeneutic efforts, then no
> voice can retain a monopoly on interpretation and no voice can try
> to limit in advance what we might learn from others. Democracy
> thus turns out to be the condition for the possibility of an enriching
> exchange of insight. Democratic conditions act against the entrench-
> ment of bigoted interpretations by offering others a fair fight as
> equals and hermeneutic conversation itself acts against the reduc-
> tion of diversity by allowing that more than one rational interpreta-
> tion might 'win.'[13]

Democracy and pluralism are not universal principles but a conception of justice that makes sense for us given our tradition. Viewing

moral theorizing as an interpretive exercise in gaining clarification, Warnke claims that disputes between theorists constitute either differences regarding the meaning of our practices and traditions or differences over which institutions best cohere with them.

Among hermeneutical philosophers, postmodernists, and moral antitheorists, there is a certain overlap of views that warrants attention. Notwithstanding important differences among the authors mentioned above (as well as numerous other thinkers within these schools), a degree of consensus has emerged between them: first, an opposition to foundationalist moral and political theories; second, an accentuation of practical over theoretical reasoning; third, a conception of normative justification as a nonformal demonstration of coherence between moral beliefs and settled convictions, tradition, or a final vocabulary; fourth, an emphasis on egalitarian communication, democracy, openness, plurality, and so on.[14] The third point — the main point of contention between universalists and proponents of a variety of positions variously termed communitarian, hermeneutical, neo-Aristotelian, pragmatic, and postmodern — faces serious difficulties. These pertain primarily to the degree of force social criticism may claim when it takes as its object institutions or norms that fall outside the "boundary" of local culture and when local solidarities harden into dogma.

A further difficulty is that when questions of justification arise the hermeneutical philosophers mentioned above frequently speak to a different issue.[15] The question of what philosophical reasons can be offered in defense of a moral belief is often transformed into the issue of where such beliefs have their historical roots: "Why ought one to believe X?" becomes "Where does the belief in X come from?" If X has been appropriated from tradition, then X warrants belief. Typically, this sort of answer is accompanied by an expression of skepticism about an autonomous, a priori rationality — which, it is asserted, must be presupposed should we wish to distinguish between the two questions. However, collapsing the questions risks making tradition a new foundation for moral claims.

Gadamer himself has been careful in his rehabilitation of tradition to avoid making appeals to tradition into philosophical justifications *per se*. His thesis that tradition is a source of understanding is never collapsed into the view that tradition is itself a philosophical justification for those beliefs that are in need of such justification. In his debate with Habermas, Gadamer writes, "Tradition is no proof and validation of something, in any case not where validation is demanded by reflection. But the point is this: where does reflection demand it? Everywhere? I would object to such an answer on the grounds of the finitude of human existence and the essential particularity of reflection."[16] Gadamer acknowledges that pointing out the customary nature of a moral belief does not always suffice as a justification. Regrettably, Gadamer does not address the questions that this inevitably raises: under what conditions is it necessary to seek a philosophical justification for traditional moral beliefs, and what form does such justification take?

An exhaustive answer to the first question may not be possible, but a partial answer may suffice. There are conditions in which we are forced to question our commitment to traditions. We may come to believe that elements of the belief system that has been handed down to us deserve to be rejected, perhaps as a result of our participating in more than one tradition — a common occurrence, particularly within multicultural societies. Experiencing conflicting demands on our loyalties from different traditions constitutes the normal course of experience for persons in many areas of the world today. Under such conditions, questions of justification will inevitably arise. We want to know which tradition most deserves our continued loyalty and which ought to be reformed or abandoned.

Similar difficulties arise when we attempt to justify moral claims by appealing to communal practices, which frequently produce conflicting or ambiguous demands. There are times when entire communities encounter difficulties with which conventional practices are unable to cope; either our moral lives lack orientation or face too many conflicting orientations. Pluralistic societies face a plethora of norms and demands for our loyalties, each arising from tradition or some measure of consensus. While resolutions to all such conflicts are not to be expected from moral philosophy, there are numerous questions that those of us who regard the realm of practice as primary must take seriously: in cases of conflict, which local practices deserve priority and which require modification? Which practices ought to be abandoned entirely, and for what sorts of reasons? To what could the social critic appeal in determining this except to other local practices and traditions that may themselves deserve to be put in abeyance? Recognizing the limits of reflection does not relieve philosophers of the responsibility of resolving issues of this kind.

It is necessary not to renounce all justificatory appeals to local consensus and tradition but to place constraints on norms thus generated, constraints fashioned by a conception of universal right. A universal theory of justice makes it possible to adjudicate certain kinds of moral conflict by establishing constraints on local institutions and practices of power. Without reintroducing totalizing perspectives, a hermeneutical theory of justice may articulate principles that will enable the critic not only to interpret the meaning of our settled convictions but to decide under what conditions they should be rejected. Differences of principle can sometimes be analyzed as interpretive differences concerning the significance of local traditions, but sometimes they cannot. Often these differences pertain not to what forms of interaction befit us as inheritors of modern Western culture but what forms of interaction befit us as human beings.

Between Gadamer and Habermas

Hermeneutic criticism is fully compatible with a universalist and rights-based morality, and acknowledging the primacy of practice need not entail abandoning theory. Normative theory appropriately takes its bearings not from an autonomous, a priori rationality but from the realm of practice itself and its aim is the explicit comprehension, critique, and reform of social practices. This theory of justice, while liberal in orientation, incorporates key elements in the thought of both Gadamer and Habermas. The former's analysis of hermeneutic experience and the latter's communicative ethics ought both to be read as elaborations of Hegel's dialectic of lordship and bondage described in the *Phenomenology of Spirit*. From this common basis may be fashioned a liberal conception of justice that prioritizes mutual recognition, openness, respect, and universal freedom. Thematizing the normative dimension implicit to hermeneutic dialogue generates a (classical) liberal conception of right. The conclusions reached by this line of argument lead us to a position likewise congenial to philosophical hermeneutics and communicative ethics — a position, as it were, between Gadamer and Habermas.[17]

One of the objections against normative theories is that they do not serve any function that could not be as well served without them.[18] As opponents of theory have forcefully argued, some of the traditional aims of moral theory and the foundationalist project in general ought to be discarded. In particular, moral theorizing should not generate procedures for determining the proper course of behavior in given cases of moral conflict. This manner of theorizing, represented by utilitarianism, contractarianism, and Kantian deontology, presupposes an abstract and autonomous rationality which has no place outside of a foundationalist, epistemology-centered conception of philosophy. In modeling moral rationality on mathematical and scientific methods, such views overlook the essentially practical nature of normative appraisal and gloss over important and ineluctable complexities of moral conduct.

If theory cannot supply formal procedures for resolving all moral conflicts, neither can it eliminate the need for practical judgment. Ethical reasoning has a concrete specificity that can never be entirely mapped in theoretical categories. Evaluative judgments do not lend themselves to tidy systematization primarily because they do not all derive from a common source. Neither can moral theory prescribe a particular way of life or conception of the good. The classical conception of ethics as a systematic answer to Socrates's question "How should one live?" was an overly ambitious view of what moral philosophy could achieve. Questions of the good cannot be resolved philosophically — so much may be conceded to the antitheorists. A general answer to this question eludes moral theorists because the way in which one approaches this question is inseparable from one's self-understanding as an individual and as a member of one or more communities. There is no method for adjudicating conflicting conceptions of the good that stem from conflicting and philosophically undecidable self-understandings, personal aspirations, and beliefs about the meaning that our lives hold for us.

The essential plurality of traditions, self-understandings, and personal aspirations may rule out a universal theory of the good life, but it does not preclude a universal theory of justice. The difficulties encountered above that arise from basing justice considerations on local traditions provide reasons to inquire into the possibility of formulating a universal theory of justice, one that would inform critical reflection without falling back into foundationalism. Principles of justice are properly rooted not in the settled convictions or final vocabulary of a community but in a universal conception of humanity. A theory of this kind would make it possible to adjudicate conflicts between local solidarities and institutions and universal requirements of justice. Such a theory would constitute an historically conscious universalism, one that recognizes that morality remains tied in some measure to tradition as well as the need for critical perspective on the same tradition.

A historically conscious universalism takes up residence between the localism of a Rorty, a Lyotard, or a Foucault, and the abstract rationalism of a Plato, a Kant, or a Hobbes. While hermeneutics forswears an autonomous, a priori rationality together with the quest for moral certainty, it opposes with equal vigor conceptions of morality that so closely link questions of justification to community that the perspective available for critical reflection is lost. Subverting these dichotomies entails a rejection of the traditional subordination of practice to theory and a recognition of the primacy of practice. The traditional view that in order to critique practices the theorist must occupy a perspective transcending the realm of practice altogether may be replaced with a conception of theoretical rationality that is subsequent to practice in the sense that it recognizes the reflective character of social practices and does not assert the need to ground them in a metaphysical conception. It represents a practice-immanent mode of moral theorizing. Rather than subordinating practice (conceived since Plato as defective, contingent, and merely empirical) to theory (conceived since Plato as unconditioned, pristine, and transcendental), the practice-immanent view takes the domain of practice as its starting point.

The aim of a theory that is immanent to practice is twofold. It informs social criticism, first, by fashioning an explicit understanding of a given practice and, second, by appraising conduct in light of this understanding. To exist as a being-in-the-world includes involvement in an array of practices, and this involvement is never without some understanding of what a practice aims to achieve, what kinds of action are appropriate to it, and what constitutes competent performance. To engage in a practice such as commerce, for instance, is to know something about the exchange of goods and services, to know what kinds of behavior to expect from other economic agents, to have particular ends in view, and to know of means instrumental in achieving these ends. This kind of understanding is usually tacit and consists primarily of practical know-how. The first service that theory can render is to thematize this practical know-how. It endeavors to gain an explicit comprehension of what we are doing when we engage in a practice — what actions characterize its performance, what aims are in view, what rules or principles are operative in the practice, and so on. Theorizing at this stage is a phenomenological or descriptive enterprise, focusing on gaining an explicit understanding of a practice. Philosophical hermeneutics is an example of a theory of this kind, attempting as it does to gain a reflective awareness of the practice of interpretation, its conditions of possibility, its limits, etc. As Gadamer expresses it, "Hermeneutics has to do with a theoretical attitude toward the practice of interpretation, the interpretation of texts, but also in relation to the experiences interpreted in them and in our communicatively unfolded orientations in the world. This theoretic stance only makes us aware reflectively of what is performatively at play in the practical experience of understanding."[19]

The second aim of theory construction is to gain critical perspective on the manner in which practices are conducted. In light of a thematic understanding of a practice, theoretical rationality formulates principles for appraising action. It supplements knowledge we already possess with principles for assessing conduct and, sometimes, methods for successfully attaining particular ends. Theoretical knowledge also enables us to challenge our practical know-how by demonstrating how it may fail to bring about the ends that the practice aims to achieve. In articulating the rules and principles already operative (prereflectively) within practices, theorizing makes it possible to reorient, or even radically overhaul, the conduct of those practices.

To illustrate: hermeneutical theory may not only gain an understanding of the practice of interpretation but enable a principled assessment of particular interpretations. Phenomenological analysis of the practice of understanding (its conditions of possibility, limits, etc.) may be supplemented with principles, such as the hermeneutic circle and the principle of coherence, useful in determining when our interpretive efforts have been successful. Principles of this kind make it possible, within limits, to adjudicate interpretive conflicts. While no amount of theorizing will generate formal procedures for interpretation, hermeneutical theory may uncover principles that are already prereflectively at play in the interpretive process, and thematizing these may inform the course of interpretation and in many cases challenge accepted readings.

Practice-immanent theorizing aids reflection by gaining a comprehensive understanding of a practice and formulating principles for the direction or assessment of conduct.[20] Of course, human understanding — including theoretical understanding — never achieves completeness or finality. The aim of theoretical understanding is not to gain a totalized perspective on human practices — something that presupposes an impossible "external" point of view — but to articulate a practice in explicit terms. As an immanent mode of theorizing, it views a practice from within, analyzing its internal constitution and the actions and principles that distinguish it as a practice.

Theoretical understanding is especially mindful of the teleological structure of practices. A practice may be understood as a complex of action types displaying a variety of interrelations and an important element of sociality. To engage in a practice is to participate in certain social relationships and to observe particular rules of interaction. These actions, relationships, and constraints have a common orientation toward the realization of specific ends — ends defined by the practice itself. Just as individual actions are goal-oriented, practices have a teleological dimension which it is the task of theorizing to render explicit. Practices such as medicine, games, the arts, or education delimit a sphere of conduct oriented toward the realization of what Alasdair MacIntyre has called "internal goods."[21] Different internal goods belong within different complexes of interrelated activities.

As MacIntyre notes, one properly engages in a practice in order to realize the ends internal to it. The practice of competitive sports aims at achieving such internal goods as fair competition, teamwork, and sportsmanship. Political activities such as running for public office or organizing political parties are oriented in principle to the realization of just social arrangements and the public good, however these are construed. The practice of education aims at imparting knowledge and enhancing critical capacity. Not all those who participate in a practice are motivated solely or even primarily toward the realization of these internal goods. As

MacIntyre observes, individuals frequently engage in a practice for the sake of attaining external goods such as power or money. However, the practice itself — if not all the agents who participate in it — remains oriented toward specific ends, the realization of which constitutes the *raison d'être* of that practice. The specific actions, rules, and constraints that constitute a practice are subordinate to these ends and can be modified in order to more successfully attain them. The rules of a competitive sport, for instance, are periodically modified to ensure fair competition and sportsmanship, that no players receive unfair advantage, and that only the skill of the players and not extraneous factors determines the outcome of a competition. Reforms of this kind are properly undertaken in order to ensure the realization of the ends of the practice.

It is through the teleological dimension of practices that a theory that is immanent to practice may articulate principles of critique. Given an understanding of the ends toward which a practice is phenomenologically oriented, the theorist may articulate principles that have their basis in, and are a reflective expression of, these ends.[22] This may be viewed as a form of immanent criticism, albeit in a sense distinct from common usage. Immanent critique is often seen as a method of contesting norms and institutions from a standpoint internal to a particular society by exposing contradictions between the society's stated beliefs and its actual practice. This method of critique, practiced by the early Frankfurt School theorists among others, demonstrates how practices contradict standards professed by the society itself. By contrast, practice-immanent criticism speaks not from the point of view of the prevailing norms of a culture but from the standpoint of principles inherent to or performatively operative within practices themselves. This kind of immanent critique inquires into the ways and means adopted by persons in their pursuit of practical ends. While it may not generate formal methods for attaining these ends, theorizing at this stage serves an essentially critical function. As Gary Madison writes, "critical social theory can enable people to improve upon their practices by (1) showing how the means that they actually employ in the pursuit of certain goals tend to subvert these very goals themselves and (2) by showing how other means would be more effective in achieving the goals."[23] In addition to posing questions about ways and means, immanent criticism can often bring to light the ways in which extraneous factors can enter into a practice and how these may corrupt the practice itself. The introduction of extraneous ends into a practice produces a kind of distortion: education, the arts, competitive sports, and other practices are distorted when extraneous factors such as the personal desires or will to power of individuals supplant the internal goods of these practices. When distortions arise, the task of the theorist is to remind individuals of the aims that belong to their practices. This method of theorizing thus recognizes the reflective character of the practices it interprets. It recognizes that neither the practices nor the ends to which they are oriented are in need of moral justification — that they are ends in themselves and central to the manner in which we understand ourselves as moral agents.

The manner in which one engages in a practice may be criticized not only on the grounds that it fails to attain the aims of the practice or replaces them with extraneous ends but on the grounds that it constitutes an injustice. Objecting that actions that cause harm do not represent "good sportsmanship," "good education," or "good business" does not fully capture the actions' injustice. In addition to such actions is the range of human conduct that lies outside the domain of social practices *per se* — the various instrumental actions that persons undertake in pursuing their interests. The question, then, is whether a mode of theorizing that takes the domain of practice as its point of departure and that forswears autonomous, unconditioned rationality may generate universally warranted principles of justice.

The objective of a theory of universal right is to provide social criticism with a principled framework of constraints on norms, institutions, and practices of power — principles that articulate a conception of common humanity. Justice may be conceived as a recognition of common humanity, not in the sense of recognizing the other as possessing an identical metaphysical nature as oneself but as a recognition of the other as genuinely other. A practice-immanent theory of justice must have an identifiable methodological starting point within the domain of human practices. This methodological starting point may be found in the universal human practice of communicative or dialogical understanding. To explain why, let us recall the ontological turn taken by hermeneutics in the twentieth century beginning with Heidegger's *Being and Time* and extending through Gadamer's *Truth and Method*.

In *Being and Time*, Heidegger transforms hermeneutics from a discipline that viewed understanding solely as a methodological problem for the humanities and social sciences to one that conceived of understanding as the fundamental mode of being of human existence itself. Understanding for Heidegger is not merely what we do but what we "are." It constitutes not merely a kind of human activity or a faculty of cognition but the universal and fundamental mode in which the human being orients itself and finds its way about the world. Human existence occurs against the background of an ontological "clearing," a tacit understanding of a lifeworld in which we orient ourselves in terms of finite possibilities. As finite and historical beings, we are "thrown" into a world of preexistent possibilities. Subjectivity is inseparable from this network of possibilities in terms of which we are constituted as the beings we are. Human existence is an incessant process of self-understanding and understanding the world to which we belong.

Along similar lines, Gadamer speaks of interpretive and dialogical understanding as belonging to the ontological condition of human beings. Hermeneutic dialogue is an ongoing "life process" which enlists individuals in a community of language and understanding.

> Coming to an understanding is not a mere action, a purposeful activity, a setting up of signs through which I transmit my will to others. Coming to an understanding as such, rather, does not need any tools,

in the proper sense of the word. It is a life process in which a community of life is lived out. To that extent, coming to an understanding through human conversation is no different from the understanding that occurs between animals. But human language must be thought of as a special and unique life process since, in linguistic communication, 'world' is disclosed. Reaching an understanding in language places a subject matter before those communicating like a disputed object set between them. Thus the world is the common ground, trodden by none and recognized by all, uniting all who talk to one another. All kinds of community are kinds of linguistic community: even more, they form language. For language is by nature the language of conversation; it fully realizes itself only in the process of coming to an understanding. That is why it is not a mere means in that process.[24]

It is in the practice of dialogical understanding that human beings reflectively cope with their experience of the world in general. Gaining familiarity with and orienting ourselves within a lifeworld involves articulating phenomena in language. While human existence is never without a tacit comprehension of the world, of itself and its possibilities, the "universal human task" (as Gadamer describes it) is to articulate the phenomena in dialogue. Gadamer, in speaking of "the conversation that we ourselves are" (378), urges a view of the practice of dialogue as, in a sense, constitutive of our humanity. Not merely a contingent behavior, dialogical understanding is a practice of universal scope and ontological import.

It is this complex of actions — speaking and listening, persuading and convincing, justifying and criticizing, fashioning judgments and generating consensus — that is fundamentally constitutive of human existence in the sense that it is ubiquitous to experience and underlies the entire range of human practices. While it has been customary since the Greeks to regard rational cognition — our sharing in the *logos* — as the distinguishing attribute of human beings, it is significant that the word *logos*, as Gadamer notes, carries a significance more fundamental than thought or reason — namely language.[25] As language users, our efforts to find our way about the world and to understand ourselves, to develop human relationships and lasting forms of community, are never without an important dimension of dialogical understanding. It is both the universality of its scope and its ontological import that gives communicative understanding a special place in the realm of human practices. It is, accordingly, to this practice that we may look in identifying a starting point for hermeneutical ethical theory.

Habermas also takes the practice of communication oriented toward mutual understanding as a point of departure in his theory of justice. For Habermas, language constitutes the distinguishing feature of human life. Habermas provides an interpretation of the different modes of language use, prioritizing and concentrating on communicative action. Language is not properly understood apart from the practice of communication, a central feature of which is the presence of validity claims. Habermas describes strategic action — a category of linguistic utterance that includes deception and manipulation — as derivative from communication oriented toward understanding because it involves a suspension of validity claims. Habermas's investigation thus leads him to the conclusion that communicative action has a kind of primacy relative to strategic action. An orientation toward reciprocity and consensus belongs to the nature of the communicative process and of language itself.

A theory of justice that is both universalist and practice-immanent must take as its methodological point of departure a practice that is itself universal in scope. With Habermas, I maintain that the practice of communicative understanding constitutes this point of departure. From this starting point, we may proceed along similar methodological lines to those outlined above, rendering explicit the teleological structure of communicative understanding, the ends that distinguish this practice, and the principles implicitly operative in its performance.

In commenting on *Truth and Method*, David Ingram identifies an important teleological dimension operative in Gadamer's analysis of hermeneutic understanding. Ingram writes that "the very *modus operandi* of human understanding is teleologically oriented toward a recognition of the 'thou' as one whose individuality merits an equal right to be respected and understood. Though such an attitude no doubt informs any search for new meaning, it is especially definitive of communicative understanding. Indeed, Gadamer regards reciprocity as in some sense a transcendental condition for the very possibility of human communication as such."[26] This reading arises from a section of *Truth and Method* in which Gadamer provides an analysis of historically effected consciousness. Gadamer distinguishes three modes of hermeneutic experience, or three ways in which an interpreter can encounter a text or tradition, and correlates each with a corresponding mode of interpersonal experience. For Gadamer, the I-Thou relation may be taken as paradigmatic of communicative understanding, and investigating this relation makes it possible to uncover a teleological dimension in hermeneutic practice.

The first mode of interpersonal experience Gadamer identifies is dominated by an objectivating attitude toward the other. This is a manner of encountering the other along the lines of a research subject: one seeks a knowledge of behavioral regularities as a means of predicting future action, for purposes perhaps of using the other as a means to one's ends. This is a decidedly premoral relation. Its correlative in hermeneutic experience involves a similar objectivating attitude toward tradition or the text. The interpreter investigates tradition in the detached manner of objective science, from an "external" perspective, or as subject to object. The interpreter believes that by applying the appropriate method one may extricate oneself thereby from one's historicity and gain the perspective of a neutral observer. This objectivistic manner of encountering tradition, as Gadamer puts it, "flattens out the nature of hermeneutical experience."[27] In overestimating the objectivity of its methods, this mode of hermeneutic experience overlooks the claims that tradition or the text makes on the interpreter.

The second I-Thou relation Gadamer describes includes a recognition of the other as a human being (rather than a mere object of scientific investigation), but it is a form of recognition that is without reciprocity. Here one purports to know the other in a complete and unconditioned fashion. The claims of the other are received not as truth claims but "reflectively" or from a radically distanced perspective. Because one is already in full possession of the truth, the claims of the other invariably meet with an authoritative reply. This relation remains dominated by the self-certainty of the I. Its correlative within hermeneutic experience includes a genuine but primarily antiquarian interest in the claims of tradition. One comprehends history in its otherness, but in a manner that keeps it at a distance and prevents one from learning what one did not already know. Being without prejudice, the interpreter need rely only on technique and not entertain the possible truth value of the traditionary claim.

It is only in the third I-Thou relation that the teleological dimension of communicative understanding becomes visible. Characterizing this as the "highest" form of hermeneutic experience, Gadamer describes a relation of reciprocity and mutual recognition. Here the other is encountered in a manner befitting human beings. This relation is characterized not by dogmatic self-certainty, but by a condition of openness and a recognition of the possibility of learning from the other. In a passage with unmistakeable ethical implications, Gadamer writes:

> In human relations the important thing is, as we have seen, to experience the Thou truly as a Thou — i.e., not to overlook his claim but to let him really say something to us. Here is where openness belongs. But ultimately this openness does not exist only for the person who speaks; rather, anyone who listens is fundamentally open. Without such openness to one another there is no genuine human bond. Belonging together always also means being able to listen to one another. When two people understand each other, this does not mean that one person 'understands' the other. Similarly, 'to hear and obey someone' does not mean simply that we do blindly

what the other desires. We call such a person slavish. Openness
to the other, then, involves recognizing that I myself must accept
some things that are against me, even though no one else forces me
to do so.[28]

In this relation, the I allows itself to be called into question by the
Thou. The conversational virtues of openness and mutuality — the
willingness to listen to the claims of the other with an eye to their
possible validity and to allow oneself to be led by the movement of
the dialogue rather than dominate it in the monological fashion of
the expert — are here fully manifest. Correspondingly, in hermeneutic experience, interpretive understanding culminates in what
Gadamer calls historically effected consciousness. This is a consciousness that is at once effected by tradition and aware of itself
as so effected, an awareness that precludes rendering tradition as
an object. Recognizing the contingency of its perspective, this mode
of hermeneutic consciousness resists all dogmatic privileging of
its perceptions and remains open to further conversation. In allowing its perspective to be called into question, historically effected
consciousness culminates not in methodological self-certainty but
an openness to further experience and dialogue.

Here the teleological and normative dimension of communicative understanding becomes apparent. "[T]he process of interpretation 'which we are,'" as Ingram writes, "is itself teleologically
oriented toward a state of openness and mutual recognition."[29] The
communicative process involves more than merely demonstrating
the truth of our convictions while registering the claims of others,
but includes an implicit orientation to a condition of openness and
reciprocity, a condition in which neither I nor Thou claims special
authority. Inherent to the communicative process is a common orientation to the meaning or truth of the subject matter, something
that never belongs entirely to an individual speaker but constitutes
an emerging consensus between interlocutors. Truth is brought to
light only in the dialectical movement of question and answer, assertion and reply, and it is within this movement that the condition

of mutual recognition Ingram describes becomes visible. Participants in dialogue are drawn into a common endeavor to uncover the truth of the text, a process that presupposes recognition of, openness toward, and willingness to be called into question by the other. The practice of dialogical understanding presupposes not only an anticipation of truth but an important normative dimension as well. This normative dimension constitutes at once a condition of the possibility of communicative understanding and its implicit telos. It is an orientation without which the dialogical process is distorted and ceases to be the practice that it is.

Gadamer's analysis of hermeneutic experience takes its bearings from Hegel's dialectic of lordship and bondage. The themes of recognition and alterity have their roots here, and it is in light of Hegel's dialectic that the teleological and normative dimension of hermeneutic practice is best understood. What Gadamer characterizes as an orientation implicit within the communicative process Hegel describes as a resolution in the struggle between lord and bondsman. Consciousness of self emerges only in the "life and death struggle" between contesting subjects, each of whom comes to realize that in order for the I to be conscious of itself it must receive confirmation from the other. The struggle for sovereignty between lord and bondsman is ultimately self-canceling since in the struggle neither receives the confirmation that each requires. Mutual recognition is the resolution of this struggle; each gains from the other an acknowledgment of autonomous self-consciousness, an acknowledgment essential to the constitution of the self.

It is here that we identify the normative dimension of Hegel's dialectic. In social relations, recognition must be mutual and freedom universal. In the struggle between lord and bondsman, both discover not only that recognizing the other is prerequisite to autonomous self-consciousness, but that one's own freedom is inseparable from the freedom of all. Hegel's narrative of recognition, as Richard Bernstein points out, generates an ethical demand that

universal freedom, autonomy, and equality between persons replace domination in its various forms.

> It becomes clear that Recognition for Hegel is not 'mere' recogni-
> tion, not simply an abstract cognitive awareness. Recognition comes
> to mean encountering and fully experiencing the other itself as a
> free, independent being. And this requires that the other self-
> consciousnesses that we confront *become* free and independent. We
> achieve and recognize our freedom in the fully recognized freedom
> of other self-consciousnesses. Politically this means that our free-
> dom is *mutually* bound up with the concrete realization of the free-
> dom of others — indeed with the freedom of all 'individual
> self-consciousnesses.' All projects to achieve individual freedom
> that do not foster the universal freedom of all self-consciousnesses
> are doomed to failure.

The practice of communicative understanding is oriented toward
recognition of others as persons and toward respecting the freedom of all. Justice, then, is a practical manner of recognizing the
individual as a free and autonomous agent. Recognizing the other
as an other means that we adopt a disposition in ethical relations,
as Stuart Hampshire puts it, "to treat all men and women alike in
certain respects, in recognition of their common humanity," or in
Kantian language, respect for persons as ends in themselves. Herein
lies the normative core of hermeneutic universalism.[30]

Habermas also conceives of communicative action as oriented
toward a condition of mutual recognition. Reminiscent of Gadamer's phenomenology of hermeneutic experience, communicative
ethics constitutes an application of Hegelian themes of recognition
and alterity as well as the Kantian conception of respect. There is
thus important common ground between a theory of justice inspired
by philosophical hermeneutics and the communicative ethics of
Habermas: both may be read in light of these Hegelian and Kantian notions, both identify the practice of communicative understanding as the appropriate point of departure for a universalist

normative theory, and both seek to render explicit the normative dimension or pragmatic presuppositions of the communicative process. Communicative ethics reconstructs the presuppositions of communicative action. "Communicative competence" possesses a universal core of presuppositions and rules, some of which function as normative conditions of discourse. Anyone who engages in the practice of communication, Habermas maintains, has always already presupposed certain principles of argumentation, rules that no speaker may contradict without falling into a performative contradiction. Habermas writes, "Briefly, the thesis that discourse ethics puts forth . . . is that anyone who seriously undertakes to participate in argumentation implicitly accepts by that very undertaking general pragmatic presuppositions that have a normative content. The moral principle can then be derived from the content of these presuppositions of argumentation. . . ."[31] Habermas's analysis of communicative action brings to light substantive moral principles that are already performatively at play in that practice and that are accepted by all speakers by virtue of their involvement in it.[32] These principles are not imposed on argumentation from without but are already operative (prereflectively) within it. These moral principles make communicative action the practice it is; were they not operative in our various acts of speaking and arguing, such acts would belong instead to the domain of strategic action.

The philosopher whose investigation of the I-Thou relation has received perhaps the greatest attention in recent years is Emmanuel Levinas. Levinas's phenomenology of the Other diverges from Gadamer's account in at least one important respect that is worth noting. This is the ethical primacy that Levinas awards to the Other (significantly, in the uppercase) rather than to the I or, as Gadamer prefers, to the relation itself. For Gadamer, the dialectical reciprocity between self and other prevents the ethical relation from deteriorating into one of mastery and servitude — a reciprocity that finds political-legal expression in the principle of equal rights — while

Levinas adamantly reserves moral priority for the Other. Its impetus is plain; to avoid the totalitarian implications of rampant egoism (an egoism ostensibly underlying many of the most profound evils of modern times) the Other becomes the rightful — and sole — source of ethical imperatives. This echoes a familiar theme in postmodern thought, the imperative to avoid the reduction of difference to sameness, divergence to convergence, and so on. Alterity must not be reduced to ipseity, nor the imperative of recognition to the self-regard of the I.

Yet, as I have elsewhere remarked,[33] Levinas's strategy for eluding such dangers is itself dangerous, and perhaps no less so than the forms of domination to which it is ostensibly opposed. When the relation of self and other is nonreciprocal, or when reciprocity itself is interpreted as a ruse of egoism, the prospect emerges of yet another class structure within ethical relations. Genuine equality, as Gadamer recognizes, is premised necessarily on a reciprocity between self and other in which both are coclaimants of the rights each would demand for itself. The recognition that Hegel insists must be reciprocal, if it is to be recognition at all, at times assumes for Levinas the quality of a one-way relation. The Other, or "the face of the Other," assumes an authoritative, superordinate position with respect to the I. The former alone becomes the source of rights or ethical imperatives while the I assumes a somewhat ambiguous position not dissimilar to subordination. If the moral intention common to Levinas's and Gadamer's phenomenologies of the I-Thou relation is to protect moral equality and personal inviolability, it is an intention that attains completion only when ethical primacy is awarded neither to the I nor the other but to the relation itself and the reciprocal recognition that is its main condition.

The values expressed in many of the writings of Rorty, Foucault, and Lyotard, equally central in the thought of Gadamer and Habermas, are an assortment of Hegelian, Kantian, and liberal themes of recognition, freedom, equality, plurality, and civility. This constellation of values is not an accidental feature of our tradition, but is implicit in the common endeavor of understanding and fashioning the social world to which we belong. Such principles supply social criticism with a moral framework for the assessment of power and social phenomena generally, whether located within our lifeworld or outside it. Without formally determining the course of reflection, principles guide our attention to the salient features of moral contexts. They permit us to inquire whether a given instance of power respects the dignity of individuals, whether a traditional norm respects the equality of persons, whether public policy is representative of the general will, or whether political institutions protect the freedom of the individual or violate it in promoting sectarian interests.

These themes are especially prominent in the liberal tradition. In this tradition, justice is conceived in terms of the conversational virtues and practices are governed by respect for persons as ends in themselves. In liberalism the status of the other is identical in principle to that of the I: self and other are moral equals as well as equals before the law. Liberal principles are animated by a conception of human beings freely choosing their values within a framework of individual rights. In this tradition, identifying the limits of what one may do in relation to the other — the extent to which one's actions may influence, govern, or interfere with another's freedom — constitutes not one moral consideration among others but (as John Stuart Mill expresses it) "the principal question in human affairs."[34] The principal question of liberal justice concerns the limits of power not only in relations between persons but between persons and institutions. Liberalism delimits (in however approximate a fashion) a sphere of action in which all persons are at liberty to pursue self-chosen ends without interference from others or the state. Its principles express an ideal of civil association in which integrity is universally respected. While principles of freedom, equality, and recognition are not exclusive to liberal doctrine, their nonliberal interpretations (from both the left and the right) are often self-negating because they entail unequal levels of obligation and formidable regulatory power, engendering new forms of power no less objectionable than those they would displace.

Thus, the normative dimension of hermeneutic practice finds its most complete expression in liberal morality alone.[35] This normative dimension is neither a fully realizable end-state (such as an ideal speech situation) or the substantive outcome of unconstrained communication. The substantive outcome of dialogue, of course, cannot be anticipated philosophically. The principles that constitute the implicit telos of hermeneutic practice constitute not the anticipated outcome of actual communicative exchanges (principles that, as if by an invisible hand, are destined to generate consensus), but the telos that the practice itself is phenomenologically oriented toward attaining. Principles of freedom, openness, respect, and so on, make communicative exchanges possible and may or may not generate actual consensus in the course of debate. Their philosophical legitimacy rests not on the likelihood of their being agreed upon in the course of debate but upon their status as conditions of the possibility of debate itself.

In sum, normative theory provides an invaluable service to social criticism by providing it with a principled framework. While theory can never eliminate interpretive conflict or the need for practical judgment, it informs interpretation and judgment by disposing reflection to the salient features of moral contexts and by placing constraints on what may reasonably pass for justice in our practices. A theory of justice at once universalist and immanent to practice identifies the implicit teleological dimension and normative conditions of the practice of communicative understanding and articulates these as principles of universal right. Without constituting a complete resolution of the debate between philosophical hermeneutics and critical theory, this conception of justice is an important, if limited, point of convergence between these two frequently antagonistic schools of thought. Both seek to reconcile the need for critique with a recognition of the conditionedness of reflection, and both attempt this reconciliation by articulating an historically conscious universalism. A more complete convergence should not be expected. The vast scientific edifice Habermas constructs in his attempt to overhaul the foundations of critical theory — the reconstruction of historical materialism, the turn to evolutionary theory and Kohlbergian moral psychology — overlooks the finitude of human understanding and fashions a new totalizing perspective. This empirical bulwark cannot be reconciled with the premises of philosophical hermeneutics. In particular, Habermas's assertion that "moral philosophy depend[s] on indirect confirmation from a developmental psychology of moral consciousness,"[36] or that ethical judgments and principles are in need of scientific corroboration and are open to empirical falsification, is a claim that hermeneutical ethics does not accept. What social criticism requires is the standpoint of universality, not scientific objectivity.

Six

Conclusion

*L*iberalism has been traditionally concerned with power in the form of legalized and quasi-physical coercion, and as the possession of centralized institutions — principally the state. Socialist and Marxist states have also been designed to cope with power thus conceived — principally the power of "capital." In each instance, the aim of political institutions is to reign in the operations of power in accordance with a conception of justice. Yet what we learn regarding the ways of power from several of its more distinguished theorists is that it is an altogether ubiquitous, universal, decentralized, and ineliminable phenomenon detectable in all forms of intersubjectivity and dispersed throughout a network of practices and institutions. It is improbable that a social order could eliminate or deaden the effects of power or that any political morality could encompass and critique in totalist fashion its multifarious operations. Even Nietzsche, Foucault, and Habermas themselves encounter difficulties in their incisive philosophies of power that they are ultimately unable to overcome and that a defensible account of social criticism must overcome. The methods of genealogy and ideology critique are unable to pronounce a critique that is philosophically compelling while remaining cognizant of its conditions and limits. For this is required an ethical-political standpoint that is universalist while historically conscious, a framework of critique premised on hermeneutical principles and liberal in orientation.

In contemporary democracies it is the nature of power not to oppress in the fashion of the *ancien regime* or totalitarian states, but to surround individuals from all sides and to perpetually scrutinize, administer, discipline, and prescribe its existence. Power administers utility, fashions knowledge, and inscribes identity as much as it subjects and controls. It is a power both multifarious and of mixed intent, alternately benign and menacing; its reach extends into all regions of human existence and its effect is normalized subjectivity. The ubiquity and multifariousness of its operations pose difficulties for its critique. Insofar as the operations of power are neither reducible to a single type or intent, nor restricted to political institutions, nor exclusively negative in consequence, nor altogether eliminable, a normative critique must match the complexity and universality of its object, providing a principled framework of appraisal without pretending that its application will fashion a power-free society. The fiction of "nonhegemonic" intersubjectivity is properly replaced with a conception of justice that prizes human autonomy across a variety of domains.

Liberalism is classically conceived as the art of separation. In keeping with that conception, the critique of power does not look to the state for remedies to all issues relating to the use of power. It regards the main service of government as securing the removal not of all possible inequalities, but of inequalities in human rights. While it is currently fashionable to speak of all relations of power as "political," the liberal view insists on preserving distinctions between political and civil society as well as between the political and the ethical. Power is endemic to human practices in general, and providing for its critique lies not solely in the domain of politics, but equally within the sphere of ethics, a domain governed not by democratic procedures but principles immanent to practices.

A primary function of public institutions is to secure an optimal configuration of options from which persons may freely choose their ends. It being the nature of power to restrict options or the perception of options, it falls to state and other institutions to loosen the hold of dogmatic consciousness by creating options in as many areas of social life as possible. A political order that limits power to its rightful domain removes obstacles to individual choice on a system-wide basis and creates options in areas where persons — many of whose perceptions and preferences, owing to the workings of power, have been unduly circumscribed — may not expect to find them. The appropriate constraint on ubiquitous power is not provided by the utilitarian state or unlimited majority rule, but by the principle of autonomy together with its main condition — a protected domain of options for all persons as wide as practical conditions allow, and an educated capacity to choose. These are options not of the "positive liberty" sort, but political and civil liberties to pursue self-chosen ends with the necessary minimum of restriction. Equal freedom, not material equality or equal means, is the principle that properly governs the use of power. Equality in the latter two connotations requires formidable powers of state intervention which compound rather than alleviate the situation that increasingly finds the individual immured in conditions of utilitarian rationalization and administrative authority.

The notion of freedom that properly limits power is the liberty to pursue self-chosen ends from among as wide a set of options as conditions permit without imposing burdensome and unequal levels of obligation. Freedom is the configuration of rights that protects persons not against all misfortune but against harmful treatment. The political order that limits power to its rightful domain maximizes options without imposing unwanted burdens and restrictions for the ostensible purpose of removing hegemony. It does not counteract power by placing it under the yoke of a power more onerous still, but circumscribes its operations with a view to enlarging the field of autonomy.

The premise of a liberal order is that power is most dangerous when it is unconstrained, and that the most effective protection

against this is the separation and balance of powers. In its traditional forms, this principle is applied mainly to state institutions in
the form of the separation of powers between executive, legisla-
tive, and judicial branches of government. A similar idea is operative in the separation of church and state and the balance of power
between nations. In each case, the operative principle is that the
only effective constraint on power is power itself: a given power is
checked by a second power of roughly equal proportions which is
a de facto competitor or counterweight of the first.

A monopoly on power in any area of practice is a formula for
abuse even if all intentions for conferring power and for wielding
it are benign. The dangers associated with power's misuse are cir-
cumvented not by beneficence, but primarily by the principle of
counterweight between powers, a principle that admits of application far broader than the classical separation and balance of powers
doctrine conceived. While not eliminating relations of superordi-
nation and subordination, competition or counterweight between
powers ensures that persons possess rights of withdrawal not from
power relations generally but from particular instances of these to
which they do not freely consent.

Mindful of both the ubiquity and ineluctability of power, liberalism regards consent — not the counterfactual consent of the ideal
speech situation or the social contract, but the actual consent of
real persons — as the principled basis of power. Since power advances on multiple fronts, assumes multiple forms, and erodes
autonomy in multiple increments, a social order that limits power
to its rightful domain meets it on an equal number of fronts, expanding options in areas of both major and minor concern. In particular,
it refuses the utilitarian policy of balancing rights alongside competing values, instead viewing them as constraints on the calculus
of social utility. Further applications of these principles in both
ethical and political contexts may be identified, yet I shall end on a
general note of reiterating the imperative of limiting power across
a wide spectrum of practices in the interest of human autonomy.

Limiting power's multifarious operations requires no wholesale expansion of entitlements or democratic rule — measures that only extend the scope of existing obligations and the reach of majoritarian power — but broader applications of rights proportionate to the powers they govern.

Notes

Notes to Introduction

1. The most basic point of contention between foundationalists and nonfoundationalists is described by Evan Simpson as follows: "Foundationalism and antifoundationalism remain positions best understood by their relationship to epistemology. The one seeks, and the other dismisses the notion of, criteria defining conditions in which some beliefs are finally justified. Few deny that beliefs need foundations, that is, the more or less secure grounds which make the conclusions of argument as solid as they can be. Any pure foundationalism, however, supposes that genuine grounds for judgment are not merely confident assumptions but absolutely secure bases which are not subject to amendment, or are amenable only in the direction of greater accuracy. Only in this way could they serve as arbiters of rational judgment. This is the notion of a single, overarching, ahistorical standard against which any claim can be tested, so that it is possible in principle to decide between rival points of view" (*Anti-Foundationalism and Practical Reasoning*, 2–3).

2. This is an observation that Michael Kelly also makes in his introduction to *Hermeneutics and Critical Theory in Ethics and Politics*, vii.

Notes to Chapter One

1. Nietzsche, *Beyond Good and Evil*, 259. Following the convention in Nietzsche scholarship, I refer to section numbers rather than page numbers where appropriate.

2. Nietzsche, *On the Genealogy of Morals*, Preface, 2.

3. *Ibid.*, 3.

4. *Ibid.*, 263.

5. In *Nietzsche: Life as Literature*, Alexander Nehamas makes this observation in the following terms: "A true individual is precisely one who is different from the rest of the world, and there is no formula, no set of rules, no code of conduct that can possibly capture in informative terms what it is to be like that. There are no principles that we can follow in order to become, as Nietzsche wants us to become, unique. On the contrary, it is by breaking rules that such a goal, if it is indeed a goal at all, can ever be reached. And it is as impossible to specify in advance the rules that must be broken for the process to succeed as it is, say, to specify in advance the conventions that must be violated for a new and innovative genre in music or literature to be established. The very notion of the individual makes it impossible to say in informative terms how one can ever become that" (225).

6. Nietzsche, *Beyond Good and Evil*, 265.

7. Nietzsche, *Twilight of the Idols*, "Morality as Anti-Nature," 5.

8. Nietzsche, *On the Genealogy of Morals*, I 7.

9. *Ibid.*, III 15.

10. *Ibid.*, II 16.

11. The phenomenon of left Nietzscheanism is remarkable in view of the vast portions of Nietzsche's writings that directly bear — virtually never in a favorable light — upon the various "emancipatory" movements of the left that he plainly despises. Left Nietzscheans habitually gloss over these texts in favor of other passages that, once removed from their context and from the larger frame of Nietzsche's thought, appear to lend support to their political views.

12. Nietzsche, *Twilight of the Idols*, "Expeditions of an Untimely Man," 38.

13. Nietzsche, *On the Genealogy of Morals*, III 12.

14. Nietzsche, *The Will to Power*, 259.

15. *Ibid.*, 259.

16. Nietzsche, *Twilight of the Idols*, "The 'Improvers' of Mankind," 1.

17. Nietzsche, *Beyond Good and Evil*, 108.

Notes to Chapter Two

1. Foucault, *History of Sexuality* 1, 88–89.

2. Foucault, *Power/Knowledge*, 98.

3. Foucault, *Discipline and Punish*, 201.

4. *Ibid.*, 194.

5. Foucault, "What is Enlightenment?" 46.

6. Foucault, *Language, Counter-Memory, Practice*, 139.

7. Foucault, *Power/Knowledge*, 84.

8. As Hubert Dreyfus and Paul Rabinow write in *Michel Foucault: Beyond Structuralism and Hermeneutics*: "Subjection, domination, and combat are found everywhere he looks. Whenever he hears talk of meaning and value, of virtue and goodness, he looks for strategies of domination. . . . Instead of origins, hidden meanings, or explicit intentionality, Foucault the genealogist finds force relations working themselves out in particular events, historical movements, and history" (109).

9. Foucault, *Politics, Philosophy, Culture*, 124.

10. See Foucault, "On Power" in *Politics, Philosophy, Culture*, 108.

11. Foucault, *Power/Knowledge*, 62.

12. *Ibid.*, 81.

13. Dreyfus and Rabinow, *Michel Foucault*, 107.

14. Along with Nietzsche, Ricoeur mentions Marx and Freud as the main figures in the hermeneutics of suspicion. Both Marx and Freud may well be read as essentialists with respect to the meaning of the phenomena they investigate. Whether this is how suspicious hermeneutics is properly construed, however, is addressed in chapter four.

15. In Hoy, *Foucault: A Critical Reader*, 98.

16. A commitment to equality is also important since power is invariably a relation of inequality between persons.

17. In Hoy, *Foucault: A Critical Reader*, 93.

18. In Dreyfus and Rabinow, *Michel Foucault*, 216.

19. At times, Foucault appears to defend a quasi-value-neutrality for genealogy in spite of his stated opposition to value-free social inquiry. In a late interview, he states that "in most of these analyses, people are not told what they ought to be, what they ought to do, what they ought to believe and think. What they do rather is to bring out how up till now social mechanisms had been able to operate, how the forms of repression and constraint had acted, and then, it seems to me, people were left to make up their own minds, to choose, in light of all this, their own existence" (*Politics, Philosophy, Culture*, 50). Also see *Remarks on Marx*, 172.

20. See Habermas, *The Philosophical Discourse of Modernity*, 266–93.

21. David Hoy offers this reading in his introduction to *Foucault: A Critical Reader*, 13–14.

22. Bernstein, *The New Constellation*, 160.

23. In Dreyfus and Rabinow, *Michel Foucault*, 231.

24. Bernstein adds that the concept of danger is itself an evaluation, one intelligible only from particular standpoints: "For we might say that the very notion of danger is itself *value-laden* — dangers for whom? Dangers from

whose perspective? Why are these dangers 'dangerous'? There is something comparable to an interpretative or hermeneutical circle here. For the very specification of what are taken to be dangers or the unique dangers of modernity itself only makes sense from an interpretative perspective — one which involves an *evaluation* of our situation, not just a 'neutral' description but an evaluative description" (*The New Constellation*, 158).

25. In Dreyfus and Rabinow, *Michel Foucault*, 216.

26. Foucault, *Politics, Philosophy, Culture*, 122.

27. I have in mind such figures as William James and John Dewey, as well as other philosophers who demonstrate a commitment to the primacy of practice such as Gadamer and Habermas.

28. In Dreyfus and Rabinow, *Michel Foucault*, 237; Nietzsche, *The Gay Science*, 290; in Dreyfus and Rabinow, *Michel Foucault*, 236.

Notes to Chapter Three

1. Instrumental rationality, as it is spoken of by critical theorists, is a formalist, utilitarian, and scientific mode of rationality oriented toward the attainment of technical mastery in a variety of domains. Arising from mathematics and the experimental sciences, this type of reasoning is dominated by the application of formal techniques instrumental in achieving technical mastery not only in the experimental sciences but within social and political affairs as well. This mode of rationality became one of the principal objects of critique in the early writings of the Frankfurt School theorists, most notably Max Horkheimer and Theodor Adorno. The primary target of this line of criticism was the manner in which instrumental rationality, with its fascination with technical problem-solving and the domination of nature, had encroached upon the social and political domain, and threatened to subject human beings to newer and more pervasive forms of domination.

2. Habermas, *Logic of the Social Sciences*, 172.

3. *Ibid.*, 173–74.

4. Habermas, *Theory and Practice*, 32.

5. Habermas, "On Systematically Distorted Communication," 209.

6. Habermas, *Logic of the Social Sciences*, 180.

7. Habermas, *Knowledge and Human Interests*, 214.

8. McCarthy, *Critical Theory of Jürgen Habermas*, 196.

9. Habermas, *Knowledge and Human Interests*, 228.

10. Interestingly, since Habermas's debate with Gadamer in the late 1960s and early 1970s — a debate in which the project of modeling a critical theory of society upon psychoanalytic methodology was a main point of

contention — Habermas's discussion of this early project and of psychoanalysis in general has been minimal. The reader interested in the development of Habermas's thought may well wonder what has become of this project, and indeed whether Habermas has renounced it. In the absence of a published recantation, however, one must assume that his interests have simply taken a different turn.

11. This example is taken from David Held's *Introduction to Critical Theory*, 186.

12. Freud, *Civilization and its Discontents*, 338.

13. In Habermas's terminology, "reconstruction" signifies the overhauling of a theory in such a way as to enable it better to achieve its original aims.

14. Habermas, *Communication and the Evolution of Society*, 140.

15. *Ibid.*, 148.

16. Kohlberg's six stages of moral judgment are as follows:

"Level A. Preconventional Level

Stage 1. The Stage of Punishment and Obedience
Content: Right is literal obedience to rules and authority, avoiding punishment, and not doing physical harm.
Stage 2. The Stage of Individual Instrumental Purpose and Exchange
Content: Right is serving one's own or other's needs and making fair deals in terms of concrete exchange.

Level B. Conventional Level

Stage 3. The Stage of Mutual Interpersonal Expectations, Relationships, and Conformity
Content: The right is playing a good (nice) role, being concerned about the other people and their feelings, keeping loyalty and trust with partners, and being motivated to follow rules and expectations.
Stage 4. The Stage of Social System and Conscience Maintenance
Content: The right is doing one's duty in society, upholding the social order, and maintaining the welfare of society or the group.

Level C. Postconventional and Principled Level

Stage 5. The Stage of Prior Rights and Social Contract or Utility
Content: The right is upholding the basic rights, values, and legal contracts of a society, even when they conflict with the concrete rules and laws of the group.
Stage 6. The Stage of Universal Ethical Principles
Content: This stage assumes guidance by universal ethical principles that all humanity should follow."

Kohlberg, *Essays on Moral Development*, 1, 409–12.

17. *Ibid.*, 170.

18. *Ibid.*, 170. The assumption of metaethical formalism is defended by

Kohlberg primarily (in fact, almost exclusively) by pointing out what he considers to be the shortcomings of opposed positions. He fully acknowledges that with respect to his metaethical assumptions, "we have argued largely by pointing out the difficulties inherent in adopting the opposed position. In the case of metaethical formalism, we know of no systematic statement of an opposed position" (*Essays on Moral Development* 2, 295–96). The oddness of this latter remark of Kohlberg's will be more than a little apparent to the many discontents of ethical foundationalism and formalism. The contemporary literature is replete with systematic statements of opposed positions, and this includes the present work.

19. Kohlberg, *Essays on Moral Development* 1, 276.

20. *Ibid.*, 172.

21. See *Ibid.*, 192 and 252. Kohlberg has written that his empirical research to date has not uncovered a single "longitudinal subject" at stage six (see *Ibid.*, 100). His examples of stage six individuals (notably Socrates and Martin Luther King) are either historical figures or individuals who have received formal philosophical training. "Stage 6," he writes, "is perhaps less a statement of an attained psychological reality than the specification of a direction in which, our theory claims, ethical development is moving" (*Ibid.*, 100).

22. *Ibid.*, 178.

23. Habermas, *Moral Consciousness and Communicative Action*, 39. Habermas is here quoting from Kohlberg's *Essays on Moral Development* 1, 178.

24. See Kohlberg, *Essays on Moral Development* 2, 218.

25. Epistemological critique was, of course, a more central concern in this debate than normative critique. However, in view of critical theory's practical intent and its preoccupation with moral and political epistemology, much of this debate is directly relevant to our concerns here.

26. Gadamer, *Philosophical Hermeneutics*, 41. The parenthetical remark in this passage is of considerable importance in Gadamer's critique. I shall return to the social critic's participation within a particular horizon of interpretation in chapter four.

27. Kohlberg, *Essays on Moral Development* 1, 254; Habermas, "A Philosophico-Political Profile," 12.

28. Habermas, "Justice and Solidarity," 34. The fourth condition of the analyst's authority in therapeutic dialogue, that such authority presupposes that the analyst be free of neurotic disturbances, involves a similar privileging of perspective by virtue of special insight, and an exempting of one's own opinion from the need for dialogical engagement.

29. Ricoeur, *Hermeneutics and the Human Sciences*, 99–100.

30. Habermas, *Moral Consciousness and Communicative Action*, 118.

Notes to Chapter Four

1. As Ricoeur expresses it: "In the same way that a text is detached from its author, an action is detached from its agent and develops consequences of its own. This autonomisation of human action constitutes the *social* dimension of action. An action is a social phenomenon not only because it is done by several agents in such a way that the role of each of them cannot be distinguished from the role of the others, but also because our deeds escape us and have effects which we did not intend" (*Hermeneutics and the Human Sciences*, 206).

2. Gadamer, *Truth and Method*, 270; *Philosophical Hermeneutics*, 9; *Truth and Method*, 276–77.

3. Gadamer writes: "It seems to me, however, that there is no such unconditional antithesis between tradition and reason. However problematic the conscious restoration of old or the creation of new traditions may be, the romantic faith in the 'growth of tradition,' before which all reason must remain silent, is fundamentally like the Enlightenment, and just as prejudiced. The fact is that in tradition there is always an element of freedom and of history itself. Even the most genuine and pure tradition does not persist because of the inertia of what once existed. It needs to be affirmed, embraced, cultivated. It is, essentially, preservation, and it is active in all historical change. But preservation is an act of reason, though an inconspicuous one. For this reason, only innovation and planning appear to be the result of reason. But this is an illusion" (*Truth and Method*, 281).

4. *Ibid.*, 389.

5. Gadamer, *Reason in the Age of Science*, 4.

6. As Gadamer puts it: "The more language is a living operation, the less we are aware of it. Thus it follows from the self-forgetfulness of language that its real being consists in what is said in it. What is said in it constitutes the common world in which we live and to which belongs also the whole great chain of tradition reaching us from the literature of foreign languages, living as well as dead. The real being of language is that into which we are taken up when we hear it — what is said" (*Philosophical Hermeneutics*, 65).

7. Gadamer, *Truth and Method*, 403.

8. "Moral language" means a particular set or family of normative concepts which typically includes a certain personal or collective self-understanding along with a wider set of beliefs and attitudes.

9. See especially MacIntyre, *After Virtue* and Stout, *Ethics After Babel*.

10. Stout, *Ethics After Babel*, 23.

11. Gadamer, *Philosophical Hermeneutics*, 7.

12. For an interesting discussion of moral imagination from the point of view of cognitive science, see Johnson, *Moral Imagination*.

13. Ricoeur, *Freud and Philosophy*, 53.

14. Aristotle, *Poetics*, 1459a.

15. Ricoeur, *Rule of Metaphor*, 4. Ricoeur also writes: "The resemblance is itself a function of the use of bizarre predicates. It consists in the coming together that suddenly abolishes the logical distance between hitherto distinct semantic fields in order to produce the semantic shock, which, in its turn, ignites the spark of meaning of the metaphor. Imagination is the apperception, the sudden glimpse, of a new predicative pertinence, namely, a way of constructing pertinence in impertinence. We could speak in this connection of a *predicative assimilation*, to stress that resemblance is itself a process, comparable to the predicative process itself. Nothing, then, is borrowed from the old association of ideas, viewed as a mechanical attraction between mental atoms. Imagining is above all restructuring semantic fields. It is, to use Wittgenstein's expression in the *Philosophical Investigations*, seeing as. . . ." (*From Text to Action*, 173).

16. "Literal" here means only habitual. In speaking of metaphor as a transferring of meaning from one domain of usage to another, it is not necessary to characterize the first usage as proper and the second as figurative. The distinction between habitual and nonhabitual is sufficient for this purpose.

17. Ricoeur, *Rule of Metaphor*, 6.

18. This proposal represents a challenge to deontology and consequentialism alike, both of which insist upon awarding exclusive moral relevance to either the motives or the consequences of human action. Against both views, the narrative conception of moral appraisal regards both motives and consequences, as well as the character of the agent, as potentially relevant considerations in forming an assessment of moral action. While in any given case, one such consideration is likely to be singled out as salient to our understanding of the action, no consideration ought to be dismissed a priori as morally irrelevant. What counts as relevant and/or salient to our judgment must be decided in the course of reflection, and not prior to it as deontologists and consequentialists propose. Many instances of moral action are best understood as occasions of further action given the serial or habitual nature of much of human conduct. An action, such as Valjean's stealing the loaf of bread, which is understood at the time of its performance as a straightforward act of theft, may come to be understood with the passage of time and in light of further actions of the agent as initiating a sequence of conduct or (in this instance) as an occasion of personal transformation. The act of theft is thus comprehended in light of the habits to which it later gave rise, thus as an occasion of further action. A primary task of moral imagination, then, is to

hold these various considerations (the short and long term consequences of the action, the effect of the action upon the character of the agent performing it, and so on) in view and to appraise conduct in light of its before and after.

19. Ricoeur, *Hermeneutics and the Human Sciences*, 170.

20. It is not necessarily the case that imaginative constructions must be novel in order to be compelling. While metaphors and narratives may deteriorate into cliché, they may also gain lasting significance.

21. Ricoeur, *Freud and Philosophy*, 34–35.

22. Gadamer, *Truth and Method*, 270.

23. Gadamer, *Philosophical Hermeneutics*, 30. Thomas McCarthy's term "normal hermeneutics" (cited in chapter three) is misleading in suggesting that the usual object domain of hermeneutics is the conscious intention of a speaker or author. This term is surprising in view of Gadamer's efforts, and those of numerous other hermeneutical philosophers, precisely to avoid reducing meaning to subjective intention.

24. Gadamer, *Philosophical Hermeneutics*, 32–33.

25. Heidegger, *Basic Writings*, 390. Heidegger, of course, defends *aletheia* as a nonmetaphysical conception of truth. My interest here is not in defending a theory of truth but in describing the relation between disclosure and concealment in a way that avoids essentialist language.

26. This also constitutes the prevailing view of application in applied ethics. Principles comprehended clearly and distinctly by theoretical reason are subsequently implemented in particular cases in a systematic and methodological fashion. Good practice is taken to be that which conforms with, or is closely determined by, theoretical principles.

27. In Rabinow and Sullivan, *Interpretive Social Science*, 125–26; Gadamer, *Truth and Method*, 310.

28. The inevitability of an infinite regress arising in formalist notions of application may be seen in Habermas, an author who has been much concerned with countering appeals by Aristotelians to *phronesis*. Defending the need for a procedural rationality governing the implementation of first order principles, Habermas has singled out the following second order principles for the direction of practical reason: first, "all relevant aspects of a case must be considered" (*Moral Consciousness and Communicative Action*, 207); second, "means should be proportionate to ends" (207); third, and more recently, Habermas has proposed that "practical reason must be informed by a principle of appropriateness. What must be determined here is which of the norms already accepted as valid is appropriate in a given case in light of all the relevant features of the situation conceived as exhaustively as possible" (*Justification and Application*, 14). Rules of this sort, Habermas believes, make possible a procedural, and hence impartial, application of first order moral

principles. The difficulty with this view, beginning with the first rule alluded to, is that the relevant aspects of a case are often far from self-evident. A third order rule is needed for determining not only what considerations qualify as relevant, but (if relevance comes in degrees) which among these relevant considerations is salient for our judgment. Formulating a general rule of this kind, of course, would be exceedingly difficult and probably impossible. The second rule above — that "means should be proportionate to ends" — would require a further rule specifying what constitutes proper proportion. Finally, what Habermas calls the principle of appropriateness appears to be an oxymoron. As it is normally conceived, appropriateness is not a formal rule-governed notion at all, but belongs within an Aristotelian vocabulary of what is "fitting" or "suitable" given the contingencies of a case, determined not by following rules but by exercising practical judgment. Were appropriateness to be refashioned as a formal principle, one would again require a further rule for determining what counts as appropriate in various types of cases, as well as a rule specifying conditions of relevance. Habermas's formalist view of application, in short, would land us in an infinite regress of rules governing rules governing rules.

29. As John Dewey notes: "There are periods in history when a whole community or a group in a community finds itself in the presence of new issues which its old customs do not adequately meet. The habits and beliefs which were formed in the past do not fit into the opportunities and requirements of contemporary life. The age in Greece following the time of Pericles was of this sort; that of the Jews after their captivity; that following the Middle Ages when secular interests on a large scale were introduced into previous religious and ecclesiastic interests; the present is preeminently a period of this sort with the vast social changes which have followed the industrial expansion of the machine age" (*Theory of the Moral Life*, 7).

30. Aristotle, *Nicomachean Ethics*, 1094b13.

31. Kant, *Critique of Judgment*, 15.

32. Gadamer and Harold Brown have both likened judgment to skillful behavior. See Gadamer, *Truth and Method*, 31; and Brown, *Rationality*, 165.

33. "[E]xplicit checking of the rules," as Brown puts it, "is not a model of competent behavior — it is a model of unskillful behavior" (*Rationality*, 157). Brown goes on to write in the same context: "When we are learning a new skill, or trying to improve a skill that we have already learned, we may pay careful attention to each of the component activities that the performance requires. But paying attention in this way impedes the smooth flow of our performance, and that flow will not be achieved until we can carry out that activity without paying attention to each act that goes into it" (161). What distinguishes the initial acquisition of a skill from competent performance is

that in the latter the rules (many of which are mere rules of thumb) are no longer "followed" but "mastered"; they are creatively adapted to the situation and more than occasionally departed from entirely. Moreover, as Brown also points out, many skills are acquired without our ever being taught an explicit set of rules (162). Language use, for instance, may indeed conform to rules, but the acquisition of this skill does not depend upon grasping and following them. Often the rules are articulated only after the skill has been acquired, and they are adhered to only as a means of perfecting an already acquired skill. And, as mentioned above, mastering this skill not infrequently involves departing from established rules of language use as a means of shedding a new light on the phenomena.

34. This point is well expressed by Charles Larmore: "But if moral judgment is not thoroughly rule-governed, it is not arbitrary either. Judgment certainly involves risk. Yet it does not resemble the flipping of a coin or a decisionistic leap of faith. Judgment we do not exercise blindly, but rather by responding with reasons to the particularity of a given situation. The fact that we are struggling to comprehend is that our perception of these reasons as indeed reasons and the response that they motivate go beyond what the general rules given in advance (as well as characteristic sentiments and training) could alone make of the situation" (*Patterns of Moral Complexity*, 20).

35. This is the doctrine that states that the meaning of a text as a whole must be understood in light of its individual parts, and that the meaning of these in turn is understood in light of the text as a whole — thus that the meaning of a text emerges in the circular movement from individual passages to the text as a whole and vice versa.

36. Gadamer and Dewey do not hold identical or nearly identical conceptions of practical rationality. I describe an area of partial, but nonetheless important, agreement between these two otherwise quite different schools of thought. I discuss the general topic of hermeneutics and pragmatism, and the relations between them, in *Theorizing Praxis*.

37. Dewey, *Reconstruction in Philosophy*, 96–97.

38. Dewey, *Theory of the Moral Life*, 141.

39. Aristotle, *Nicomachean Ethics*, 1137b12.

40. "Rationalistic logic," Dewey writes, "formerly made men careless in observation of the concrete in physical philosophy. It now operates to depress and retard observation in specific social phenomena. The social philosopher, dwelling in the region of his concepts, 'solves' problems by showing the relationship of ideas, instead of helping men solve problems in the concrete by supplying them hypotheses to be used and tested in projects of reform. Meanwhile, of course, the concrete troubles and evils remain" (*Reconstruction in Philosophy*, 191–92).

41. In Rabinow and Sullivan, *Interpretive Social Science*, 122.
42. Wittgenstein, *Philosophical Investigations*, 31.

Notes to Chapter Five

1. Lyotard and Thebaud, *Just Gaming*, 73.
2. Rorty, *Contingency, Irony, and Solidarity*, 75.
3. Richard Bernstein makes this observation in *The New Constellation*.
4. Rorty, *Contingency, Irony, and Solidarity*, 67–68.
5. Lyotard, *Just Gaming*, 94.
6. Rorty, *Philosophical Papers* 1, 30.
7. *Ibid.*, 30.
8. As Rorty puts it: "The pragmatists' justification of toleration, free inquiry, and the quest for undistorted communication can only take the form of a comparison between societies which exemplify these habits and those which do not, leading up to the suggestion that nobody who has experienced both would prefer the latter. It is exemplified by Winston Churchill's defense of democracy as the worst form of government imaginable, except for all the others which have been tried so far. Such justification is not by reference to a criterion, but by reference to various detailed practical advantages. It is circular only in that the terms of praise used to describe liberal societies will be drawn from the vocabulary of the liberal societies themselves. Such praise has to be in *some* vocabulary, after all, and the terms of praise current in primitive or theocratic or totalitarian societies will not produce the desired result. So the pragmatist admits that he has no ahistorical standpoint from which to endorse the habits of modern democracies he wishes to praise" (*Ibid.*, 29).
9. See especially Smith, *Hermeneutics and Human Finitude*; Foster, *Gadamer and Practical Philosophy*; and Warnke, *Justice and Interpretation*.
10. In *Justice and Interpretation*, Warnke takes her inspiration not only from Gadamer's hermeneutics but also from the political thought of Michael Walzer, Alasdair MacIntyre, and John Rawls, among others.
11. Smith, *Hermeneutics and Human Finitude*, xvi.
12. Warnke, *Justice and Interpretation*, 5.
13. *Ibid.*, 157.
14. This characterization is by no means intended to minimize the differences between the many philosophers who belong to these schools of thought. Undoubtedly, many do not subscribe to all four of these points, and of those who do, important areas of disagreement exist with respect to a variety of issues, not all of which can be enumerated here. What I am describing is

something of an ideal position represented, in different degrees and with different shades of emphasis, by a large number of contemporary philosophers. It describes an area of limited, but nonetheless important, convergence.

15. This observation is also made by Richard Bernstein. See Hollinger, *Hermeneutics and Praxis*, 285–87.

16. Gadamer, *Philosophical Hermeneutics*, 34.

17. It is interesting to note that since the time of their debate, Gadamer and Habermas have both taken an increasing interest in ethical questions. Albeit in sharply different ways, both have defended a notion of communicative rationality and pointed out the need for unconstrained dialogue in matters of ethics and politics. While nothing resembling a consensus has emerged between these two thinkers, what follows may indicate a general direction in which such a partial convergence could be found within moral philosophy.

18. This criticism is expressed by Cheryl N. Noble in Simpson and Clarke, *Anti-Theory in Ethics and Moral Conservatism*, and also finds expression in the writings of Foucault, Lyotard, and Rorty.

19. Gadamer, *Reason in the Age of Science*, 112.

20. A similar view of theory is defended by Gary Madison in "The Practice of Theory, The Theory of Practice." He writes: "The theoretically true is not only that which illuminates, i.e., helps us to attain to a reflective consciousness of our practices; it is also that which can help us to get a better handle on our practices, can, in other words, aid us in *changing*, improving upon our practices. The truth of theory lies always, and only, in the practical" (190–91).

21. MacIntyre, *After Virtue*, 187–89.

22. The difficulty involved in identifying a practice's teleological dimension should not be underestimated. This is often a matter of considerable controversy. Physicians, for example, are often criticized for putting the profit motive ahead of the health of their patients. They may reply that they are not only physicians but entrepreneurs, and that as such their activities are properly oriented toward profit maximization. The difficulty here stems from the fact that the professional activities of physicians appear to fall under the domain of two distinct practices: medicine and commerce. As distinct practices, medicine and commerce are oriented toward attaining very different goals, and this may well raise questions about which ought to take priority in instances of conflict between the physicians's profit motive and the well being of patients. Resolving issues of this kind would require supplementing phenomenological analysis of practices with an ethical judgment concerning which internal goods take priority in conflicts of this kind. Perhaps the most reasonable judgment in this case would be that while physicians are indeed entrepreneurs of a sort (analogous in important ways to accountants and lawyers),

and thus that the pursuit of profit is a legitimate goal, the manner in which they pursue profit is constrained by responsibilities belonging to them by virtue of their profession. Undoubtedly, more argumentation would be needed to resolve this matter thoroughly, but it is in this direction that solutions to conflicts of this kind are likely to be found.

23. Madison, "The Practice of Theory, The Theory of Practice," 201.

24. Gadamer, *Truth and Method*, 446.

25. Gadamer, *Philosophical Hermeneutics*, 59.

26. In Hollinger, *Hermeneutics and Praxis*, 45.

27. Gadamer, *Truth and Method*, 359.

28. *Ibid.*, 361.

29. In Hollinger, *Hermeneutics and Praxis*, 39.

30. Bernstein, *The New Constellation*, 303; Hampshire, *Morality and Conflict*, 136; Kant draws an important distinction in *Critique of Practical Reason* between respect and admiration. See Kant, *Critique of Practical Reason*, 79–81. Respect generates obligations to treat all persons alike in certain ways in virtue of what we share as human beings, while admiration urges us to treat individuals differently on account of their personal characteristics. Accordingly, admiration permits degrees while respect does not. It is this sense of respect that is analogous with Hegelian recognition and that deserves to be taken up in a conception of universal right. Kant's notion of respect, however, also has clearly metaphysical overtones which are dubious at best. It is less the person as such who constitutes the object of respect in Kant's view than the person as an instantiation of the moral law. It is only as a rational being choosing in accordance with, and on the basis of, the categorical imperative that one is an object of respect for Kant. It would be preferable to abandon metaphysical talk of "the moral law" and "the law made visible," and replace this with a notion of respect for persons as such.

31. Habermas, *Moral Consciousness and Communicative Action*, 197–98.

32. Gary Madison argues along similar lines in *The Logic of Liberty*. He writes: "By the very fact that people engage in discussion, they commit themselves to the principle that this is the way social issues should be resolved. That is, it is logically impossible for them, as discussants, to deny this principle. Thus, to the degree that a person engages in discussion (abstaining, by that very fact, from the use of force), he is, whether he likes it or not, affirming a fundamental, universal norm, one on which the whole liberal philosophy depends" (*The Logic of Liberty*, 266–67). Ricoeur expresses a similar view in speaking of discourse and violence as "the two opposite poles of human existence": "Violence is always the interruption of discourse: discourse is always the interruption of violence. A violence that speaks is already a violence that is trying to be in the right, that is exposing itself to the gravitational

pull of Reason and already beginning to renegue on its own character as violence. The prime example of this is that the 'tyrant' always tries to get discourse on his side. The tyrant, for Plato, is the opposite of the philosopher, the man of rational discourse. But in order to succeed tyranny has to seduce, persuade, flatter; it has never been the dumb exercise of brute force. Tyranny only puts itself across to the public by perverting language. The tyrant prefers the sophist's services to the executioner's; he needs the sophist to find words and phrases that stir up hatred and involve others ineluctably as accomplices in his crime" (*Main Trends in Philosophy*, 226).

33. See Fairfield, *Theorizing Praxis*, 156–57.

34. John Stuart Mill, *On Liberty*, 7.

35. A criticism bound to arise at this stage of the argument concerns the metaphysical and atomistic conception of the self that liberalism has traditionally presupposed, a conception (or conceptions) that has come under considerable criticism in recent decades from several schools of thought, including hermeneutics. I devote considerable attention to this problem in *Moral Selfhood in the Liberal Tradition*.

36. Habermas, *Moral Consciousness and Communicative Action*, 119.

Bibliography

Alejandro, Roberto. *Hermeneutics, Citizenship, and the Public Sphere.* Albany: State University of New York Press, 1993.

Apel, Karl-Otto. *Towards a Transformation of Philosophy.* Trans. Glyn Adey and Davis Frisby. Boston: Routledge and Kegan Paul, 1980.

Arendt, Hannah. "Freedom and Politics." In *Freedom and Serfdom: An Anthology of Western Thought*, edited by Albert Hunold. Dordrecht: D. Reidel Publishing Co., 1961.

———. *The Human Condition.* Chicago: University of Chicago Press, 1958.

Aristotle. *The Basic Works of Aristotle*, edited by Richard McKeon. New York: Random House, 1941.

Avineri, Shlomo and Avner de-Shalit, eds. *Communitarianism and Individualism.* Oxford: Oxford University Press, 1992.

Beiner, Ronald. "Do We Need a Philosophical Ethics? Theory, Prudence, and the Primacy of Ethos." *Philosophical Forum* 20 (3).

———. *Political Judgment.* Chicago: University of Chicago Press, 1983.

Benhabib, Seyla. *Critique, Norm, and Utopia: A Study of the Foundations of Critical Theory.* New York: Columbia University Press, 1986.

———. "In the Shadow of Aristotle and Hegel: Communicative Ethics and Current Controversies in Practical Philosophy." In *Hermeneutics and Critical Theory in Ethics and Politics*, edited by Michael Kelly. Cambridge: MIT Press, 1990.

Benhabib, Seyla and Fred Dallmayr, eds. *The Communicative Ethics Controversy.* Cambridge: MIT Press, 1990.

Berkowitz, Peter. *Nietzsche: The Ethics of an Immoralist*. Cambridge: Harvard University Press, 1995.

Bernauer, James and David Rasmussen, eds. *The Final Foucault*. Cambridge: The MIT Press, 1991.

Bernstein, Richard J. *Beyond Objectivism and Relativism: Science, Hermeneutics, and Praxis*. Philadelphia: University of Pennsylvania Press, 1985.

———. "From Hermeneutics to Praxis." In *Hermeneutics and Praxis*, edited by Robert Hollinger. Notre Dame: University of Notre Dame Press, 1985.

———. *The New Constellation: The Ethical-Political Horizons of Modernity/Postmodernity*. Cambridge: MIT Press, 1992.

———. "Philosophy in the Conversation of Mankind." *Review of Metaphysics*, no. 132.

———, ed. *Habermas and Modernity*. Cambridge: MIT Press, 1985.

Brown, Harold I. *Rationality*. New York: Routledge, 1988.

Buber, Martin. *I and Thou*. Trans. Walter Kaufmann. New York: Scribners, 1970.

Caputo, John D. *Radical Hermeneutics: Repetition, Deconstruction, and the Hermeneutic Project*. Bloomington: Indiana University Press, 1987.

Casey, Edward. *Imagining: A Phenomenological Study*. Bloomington: Indiana University Press, 1979.

Dallmayr, Fred R. *Polis and Praxis: Exercises in Contemporary Political Theory*. Cambridge: MIT Press, 1984.

Dallmayr, Fred R. and Thomas A. McCarthy, eds. *Understanding and Social Inquiry*. Notre Dame: University of Notre Dame Press, 1977.

Dewey, John. *Human Nature and Conduct. The Middle Works of John Dewey, Vol. 14: 1922*, edited by Jo Ann Boydston. Carbondale: Southern Illinois University Press, 1983.

———. *Liberalism and Social Action*. New York: Capricorn Books, 1963.

———. *The Quest for Certainty. The Later Works of John Dewey, Vol. 4: 1929*, edited by Jo Ann Boydston. Carbondale: Southern Illinois University Press, 1984.

———. *Reconstruction in Philosophy*. Boston: Beacon Press, 1957.

———. *Theory of the Moral Life*. New York: Irvington Publishers, 1980.

DiCenso, James J. *Hermeneutics and the Disclosure of Truth: A Study in the Work of Heidegger, Gadamer, and Ricoeur.* Charlottesville: University Press of Virginia, 1990.

Dreyfus, Hubert and Paul Rabinow. *Michel Foucault: Beyond Structuralism and Hermeneutics*, 2nd ed. Chicago: University of Chicago Press, 1982.

Dworkin, Ronald. *Taking Rights Seriously.* Cambridge: Harvard University Press, 1977.

Dyrberg, Torben Bech. *The Circular Structure of Power: Politics, Identity, Community.* New York: Verso, 1997.

Elshtain, Jean Bethke. *Democracy on Trial.* Concord: House of Anansi Press, 1993.

Fairfield, Paul. *Moral Selfhood in the Liberal Tradition: The Politics of Individuality.* Toronto: University of Toronto Press, 2000.

———. *Theorizing Praxis: Studies in Hermeneutical Pragmatism.* New York: Peter Lang Publishing, 2000.

Fay, Brian. *Critical Social Science: Liberation and its Limits.* Ithaca: Cornell University Press, 1987.

Foster, Matthew. *Gadamer and Practical Philosophy: The Hermeneutics of Moral Confidence.* Atlanta: Scholars Press, 1991.

Foucault, Michel. *Discipline and Punish: The Birth of the Prison.* Trans. Alan Sheridan. New York: Vintage Books, 1979.

———. *The History of Sexuality*, 3 vols. Trans. Robert Hurley. New York: Vintage Books, 1987, 1988, 1990.

———. *Language, Counter-Memory, Practice: Selected Essays and Interviews*, edited by Donald F. Bouchard and trans. Donald F. Bouchard and Sherry Simon. Ithaca: Cornell University Press, 1977.

———. *Politics, Philosophy, Culture: Interviews and Other Writings 1977–1984*, edited by Lawrence D. Kritzman and trans. Alan Sheridan and others. New York: Routledge, 1988.

———. *Power/Knowledge: Selected Interviews and Other Writings 1972–1977*, edited by Colin Gordon and trans. Colin Gordon, Leo Marshall, John Mepham, and Kate Soper. New York: Pantheon Books, 1972.

———. *Remarks on Marx.* Trans. James Goldstein and James Cascaito. New York: Semiotext(e), 1991.

————. "What is Enlightenment?" In *The Foucault Reader*, edited by Paul Rabinow and trans. Catherine Porter. New York: Pantheon Books, 1984.

Freeden, Michael. *The New Liberalism: An Ideology of Social Reform.* Oxford: Clarendon Press, 1978.

Freud, Sigmund. *Civilization and its Discontents.* In *Civilization, Society, and Religion.* The Pelican Freud Library, Vol. 12. Ed. Albert Dickson and trans. James Strachey. Middlesex: Penguin Books, 1985.

Gadamer, Hans-Georg. *The Enigma of Health: The Art of Healing in a Scientific Age.* Trans. Jason Gaiger and Nicholas Walker. Stanford: Stanford University Press, 1996.

————. *Hegel's Dialectic: Five Hermeneutical Studies.* Trans. P. Christopher Smith. New Haven: Yale University Press, 1976.

————. "The Hermeneutics of Suspicion." In *Hermeneutics: Questions and Prospects*, edited by Gary Shapiro and Alan Sica. Amherst: University of Massachusetts Press, 1984.

————. *The Idea of the Good in Platonic-Aristotelian Philosophy.* Trans. P. Christopher Smith. New Haven: Yale University Press, 1986.

————. *Philosophical Hermeneutics.* Ed. and trans. David. E. Linge. Berkeley: University of California Press, 1976.

————. *Plato's Dialectical Ethics: Phenomenological Interpretations Relating to the Philebus.* Trans. Robert M. Wallace. New Haven: Yale University Press, 1991.

————. "The Power of Reason." *Man and World* 3, no. 1.

————. *Praise of Theory: Speeches and Essays.* Trans. Chris Dawson. New Haven: Yale University Press, 1998.

————. "The Problem of Historical Consciousness." In *Interpretive Social Science: A Second Look*, edited by Paul Rabinow and William M. Sullivan. Los Angeles: University of California Press, 1987.

————. *Reason in the Age of Science.* Trans. Frederick G. Lawrence. Cambridge: MIT Press, 1982.

————. "Text and Interpretation." In *Hermeneutics and Modern Philosophy*, ed. Brice R. Wachterhauser. Albany: State University of New York Press, 1986.

————. *Truth and Method.* Second Revised Edition. Trans. Joel Weinsheimer and Donald Marshall. New York: Crossroad, 1989.

Gadamer, Hans-Georg and Paul Ricoeur. "The Conflict of Interpretations." In *Phenomenology: Dialogues and Bridges*, edited by Ronald Bruzina and Bruce Wilshire. New York: State University of New York Press, 1982.

Gallie, W. B. "Essentially Contested Concepts." In *The Importance of Language*, edited by M. Black. Englewood Cliffs, N. J.: Prentice-Hall, 1962.

Geraets, Theodore F., ed. *Rationality Today*. Ottawa: University of Ottawa Press, 1979.

Geuss, Raymond. *The Idea of a Critical Theory: Habermas and the Frankfurt School*. Cambridge: Cambridge University Press, 1981.

Günther, Klaus. "Impartial Application of Moral and Legal Norms: A Contribution to Discourse Ethics." In *Universalism vs. Communitarianism: Contemporary Debates in Ethics*, edited by David Rasmussen. Cambridge: MIT Press, 1990.

Gutting, Gary, ed. *The Cambridge Companion to Foucault*. Cambridge: Cambridge University Press, 1994.

Haan, Norma, Robert Bellah, Paul Rabinow, and William Sullivan, eds. *Social Science as Moral Inquiry*. New York: Columbia University Press, 1983.

Habermas, Jürgen. *Between Facts and Norms: Contributions to a Discourse Theory of Law and Democracy*. Trans. William Rehg. Cambridge: MIT Press, 1998.

———. *Communication and the Evolution of Society*. Trans. Thomas McCarthy. Boston: Beacon Press, 1979.

———. "The Hermeneutic Claim to Universality." In *Contemporary Hermeneutics: Hermeneutics as Method, Philosophy and Critique*, edited and translated by Josef Bleicher. New York: Routledge, 1980.

———. *The Inclusion of the Other: Studies in Political Theory*. Eds. Ciaran Cronin and Pablo De Greiff and trans. Ciaran Cronin and others. Cambridge: MIT Press, 1998.

———. "Justice and Solidarity: On the Discussion Concerning 'Stage 6.'"In *Hermeneutics and Critical Theory in Ethics and Politics*, edited by Michael Kelly. Cambridge: MIT Press, 1990.

———. *Justification and Application: Remarks on Discourse Ethics*. Trans. Ciaran P. Cronin. Cambridge: MIT Press, 1993.

————. *Knowledge and Human Interests*. Trans. Jeremy J. Shapiro. Boston: Beacon Press, 1971.

————. "On Systematically Distorted Communication." *Inquiry* 13 (May/June 1985).

————. *On the Logic of the Social Sciences*. Trans. Shierry Weber Nicholsen and Jerry A. Stark. Cambridge: MIT Press, 1988.

————. *Moral Consciousness and Communicative Action*. Trans. Christian Lenhardt and Shierry Weber Nicholsen. Cambridge: MIT Press, 1990.

————. *The Philosophical Discourse of Modernity: Twelve Lectures*. Trans. Frederick G. Lawrence. Cambridge: MIT Press, 1987.

————. "A Philosophico-Political Profile." *New Left Review* 151.

————. *The Structural Transformation of the Public Sphere: An Inquiry into a Category of Bourgeois Society*. Trans. Thomas Burger and Frederick Lawrence. Cambridge: MIT Press, 1991.

————. *Theory and Practice*. Trans. John Viertel. Boston: Beacon Press, 1973.

————. *The Theory of Communicative Action, Vol. 1, Reason and the Rationalization of Society*. Trans. Thomas McCarthy. Boston: Beacon Press, 1984.

Hahn, Lewis Edwin, ed. *The Philosophy of Hans-Georg Gadamer*. Chicago: Open Court, 1997.

————, ed. *The Philosophy of Paul Ricoeur*. Chicago: Open Court, 1995.

Hampshire, Stuart. *Morality and Conflict*. Cambridge: Harvard University Press, 1983.

Havas, Randall. *Nietzsche's Genealogy: Nihilism and the Will to Knowledge*. Ithaca: Cornell University Press, 1995.

Haworth, Lawrence. *Autonomy: An Essay in Philosophical Psychology and Ethics*. New Haven: Yale University Press, 1986.

Hayek, F. A. *The Constitution of Liberty*. South Bend: Gateway Editions, 1972.

————. *The Road to Serfdom*. Chicago: University of Chicago Press, 1994.

Hegel, G. W. F. *Elements of the Philosophy of Right*. Trans. H. B. Nisbet. Cambridge: Cambridge University Press, 1991.

————. *Phenomenology of Spirit*. Trans. A. V. Miller. New York: Oxford University Press, 1977.

Heidegger, Martin. *Being and Time*. Trans. John Macquarrie and Edward Robinson. New York: Harper and Row, 1962.

————. *Basic Writings*. Ed. David Farrell Krell. New York: Harper and Row, 1977.

Held, David. *Introduction to Critical Theory: Horkheimer to Habermas*. Los Angeles: University of California Press, 1980.

Hoffmaster, Barry. "Morality and the Social Sciences." In *Social Science Perspectives on Medical Ethics*, edited by G. Weisz. Boston: Kluwer Academic Publishers, 1990.

Hollinger, Robert, ed. *Hermeneutics and Praxis*. Notre Dame: University of Notre Dame Press, 1985.

Holub, Robert C. *Jürgen Habermas: Critic in the Public Sphere*. New York: Routledge, 1991.

Honneth, Axel. *The Critique of Power: Reflective Stages in a Critical Social Theory*. Trans. Kenneth Baynes. Cambridge: MIT Press, 1993.

Honneth, Axel and Hans Joas. *Communicative Action: Essays on Jürgen Habermas's The Theory of Communicative Action*. Trans. Jeremy Gaines and Doris L. Jones. Cambridge: MIT Press, 1991.

Honneth, Axel, Thomas McCarthy, Claus Offe, and Albrecht Wellmer, eds. *Cultural-Political Interventions in the Unfinished Project of Enlightenment*. Trans. Barbara Fultner. Cambridge: MIT Press, 1992.

Horkheimer, Max. *Critical Theory: Selected Essays*. Trans. Matthew O'Connell. New York: Herder and Herder, 1972.

————. *Critique of Instrumental Reason*. Trans. Matthew J. O'Connell. New York: Continuum, 1994.

Horkheimer, Max and Theodor W. Adorno. *Dialectic of Enlightenment*. Trans. John Cumming. New York: Continuum, 1991.

Hoy, David Couzens. *The Critical Circle: Literature, History, and Philosophical Hermeneutics*. Los Angeles: University of California Press, 1982.

————, ed. *Foucault: A Critical Reader*. Cambridge: Basil Blackwell, 1986.

Humboldt, Wilhelm von. *The Limits of State Action*. Ed. J. W. Burrow. Indianapolis: Liberty Fund, 1993.

Ingram, David. *Habermas and the Dialectic of Reason*. New Haven: Yale University Press, 1987.

―――. "Hermeneutics and Truth." In *Hermeneutics and Praxis*, edited by Robert Hollinger. Notre Dame: University of Notre Dame Press, 1985.

―――. *Reason, History, and Politics: The Communitarian Grounds of Legitimation in the Modern Age*. Albany: State University of New York Press, 1995.

Jaspers, Karl. *The Future of Mankind*. Trans. E. B. Ashton. Chicago: University of Chicago Press, 1961.

―――. *Nietzsche: An Introduction to the Understanding of His Philosophical Activity*. Trans. Charles F. Wallraff and Frederick J. Schmitz. Tucson: University of Arizona Press, 1966.

Johnson, Mark. *Moral Imagination: Implications of Cognitive Science for Ethics*. Chicago: University of Chicago Press, 1993.

Kant, Immanuel. *Critique of Judgment*. Trans. J. H. Bernard. New York: Hafner Press, 1951.

―――. *Critique of Practical Reason*. Trans. Lewis White Beck. New York: Macmillan, 1956.

―――. *Foundations of the Metaphysics of Morals* and *What is Enlightenment?* 2nd ed. Trans. Lewis White Beck. New York: Macmillan, 1990.

Kaufmann, Walter. *Nietzsche: Philosopher, Psychologist, Antichrist*. Princeton: Princeton University Press, 1974.

Kearney, Richard. *Poetics of Imagining: From Husserl to Lyotard*. London: Harper Collins, 1991.

Keat, Russell. *The Politics of Social Theory: Habermas, Freud and the Critique of Positivism*. Oxford: Basil Blackwell, 1981.

Kelly, Michael. Ed. *Hermeneutics and Critical Theory in Ethics and Politics*. Cambridge: MIT Press, 1990.

Kemp, T. Peter and David Rasmussen, eds. *The Narrative Path: The Later Works of Paul Ricoeur*. Cambridge: MIT Press, 1989.

Kisiel, Theodore. "The Happening of Tradition: The Hermeneutics of Gadamer and Heidegger." *Man and World* 2.

Kögler, Hans Herbert. *The Power of Dialogue: Critical Hermeneutics After Gadamer and Foucault*. Trans. Paul Hendrickson. Cambridge: MIT Press, 1996.

Kohlberg, Lawrence. *Essays on Moral Development,* 2 Vols. San Francisco: Harper and Row, 1981, 1984.

Kortian, Garbis. *Metacritique: The Philosophical Argument of Jürgen Habermas.* Cambridge: Cambridge University Press, 1980.

Kymlicka, Will. *Liberalism, Community, and Culture.* Oxford: Clarendon Press, 1989.

Larmore, Charles E. *Patterns of Moral Complexity.* Cambridge: Cambridge University Press, 1987.

————. *The Romantic Legacy.* New York: Columbia University Press, 1996.

Leonard, Stephen. *Critical Theory in Political Practice.* Princeton: Princeton University Press, 1990.

Levinas, Emmanuel. *Otherwise Than Being or Beyond Essence.* Trans. Alphonso Lingis. Boston: Martinus Nijhoff Publishers, 1981.

————. *Totality and Infinity: An Essay on Exteriority.* Trans. Alphonso Lingis. Boston: Kluwer Academic Publishers, 1991.

Lingis, Alphonso. *The Imperative.* Bloomington: Indiana University Press, 1998.

Llewelyn, John. *Beyond Metaphysics? The Hermeneutic Circle in Contemporary Continental Philosophy.* Atlantic Highlands: Humanities Press International, 1985.

Locke, John. *Two Treatises of Government.* Ed. Peter Laslett. Cambridge: Cambridge University Press, 1994.

Lukes, Steven. *Power: A Radical View.* London: Macmillan Press, 1974.

Lyotard, Jean-François. *The Differend: Phrases in Dispute.* Trans. Georges Van Den Abbeele. Minneapolis: University of Minnesota Press, 1988.

————. *The Postmodern Condition: A Report on Knowledge.* Trans. Geoff Bennington and Brian Massumi. Minneapolis: University of Minnesota Press, 1979.

Lyotard, Jean-François and Jean-Loup Thebaud. *Just Gaming.* Trans. Wlad Godzich. Minneapolis: University of Minnesota Press, 1985.

MacIntyre, Alasdair. *After Virtue: A Study in Moral Theory.* 2nd ed. Notre Dame: University of Notre Dame Press, 1984.

————. *Whose Justice? Which Rationality?* Notre Dame: University of Notre Dame Press, 1988.

MacLean, Douglas and Mills, Claudia. Eds. *Liberalism Reconsidered.* Totowa: Rowman and Allanheld, 1983.

Madison, Gary B. *The Hermeneutics of Postmodernity: Figures and Themes.* Bloomington: Indiana University Press, 1988.

————. *The Logic of Liberty.* Westport: Greenwood Press, 1986.

————. *The Phenomenology of Merleau-Ponty: A Search for the Limits of Consciousness.* Athens: Ohio University Press, 1981.

————. "Philosophy Without Foundations." *Reason Papers* 16.

————. *The Political Economy of Civil Society and Human Rights.* London: Routledge, 1998.

————. *The Politics of Postmodernity.* Boston: Kluwer Academic Publishers, 2001.

————. "The Practice of Theory, The Theory of Practice." *Critical Review* 5, no. 2.

————. *Understanding: A Phenomenological-Pragmatic Analysis.* Westport: Greenwood Press, 1982.

Madison, Gary B., Paul Fairfield, and Ingrid Harris. *Is There a Canadian Philosophy? Reflections on the Canadian Identity.* Ottawa: University of Ottawa Press, 2000.

Madison, Gary B. and Marty Fairbairn, eds. *The Ethics of Postmodernity: Current Trends in Continental Thought.* Evanston: Northwestern University Press, 1999.

Magnus, Bernd. *Nietzsche's Existential Imperative.* Bloomington: Indiana University Press, 1978.

Magnus, Bernd and Kathleen M. Higgins, eds. *The Cambridge Companion to Nietzsche.* Cambridge: Cambridge University Press, 1996.

Manent, Pierre. *An Intellectual History of Liberalism.* Trans. Rebecca Balinski. Princeton: Princeton University Press, 1994.

Markovic, Mihailo. "The Idea of Critique in Social Theory." *Praxis International* 3, no. 2.

Marx, Werner. *Towards a Phenomenological Ethics: Ethos and the Life-World.* Trans. Stefaan Heyvaert. Albany: State University of New York Press, 1992.

McCarthy, Thomas. *The Critical Theory of Jürgen Habermas.* Cambridge: MIT Press, 1989.

McIntosh, Donald. "Habermas on Freud." *Social Research* 44, no. 3.

Michelfelder, Diane P. and Richard E. Palmer, eds. *Dialogue and Deconstruction: The Gadamer-Derrida Encounter*. Albany: State University of New York Press, 1989.

Mill, John Stuart. *On Liberty*. Ed. David Spitz. New York: W. W. Norton and Co., 1975.

Misgeld, Dieter. "Discourse and Conversation: The Theory of Communicative Competence and Hermeneutics in the Light of the Debate Between Habermas and Gadamer." *Cultural Hermeneutics* 4.

Mouffe, Chantal. "Democratic Citizenship and the Political Community." In *Dimensions of Radical Democracy: Pluralism, Citizenship, Community*, edited by Chantal Mouffe. New York: Verso, 1992.

Mueller-Vollmer, Kurt, ed. *The Hermeneutics Reader*. New York: Continuum, 1988.

Nagele, Rainer. "Real and Ideal Discourses: Freud, Habermas and the Dialectic of Enlightenment." *New German Critique*, no. 22.

Nehamas, Alexander. *Nietzsche: Life as Literature*. Cambridge: Harvard University Press, 1985.

Nietzsche, Friedrich. *Beyond Good and Evil: Prelude to a Philosophy of the Future*. Trans. Walter Kaufmann. New York: Vintage Books, 1989.

―――. *Daybreak: Thoughts on the Prejudices of Morality*. Trans. R. J. Hollingdale. Cambridge: Cambridge University Press, 1982.

―――. *The Gay Science*. Trans. Walter Kaufmann. New York: Vintage Books, 1974.

―――. *On the Genealogy of Morals* and *Ecce Homo*. Trans. Walter Kaufmann and R. J. Hollingdale. New York: Vintage Books, 1969.

―――. *Human, All Too Human: A Book for Free Spirits*. Trans. Marion Faber and Stephen Lehmann. Lincoln: University of Nebraska Press, 1984.

―――. *On the Genealogy of Morals* and *Ecce Homo*. Ed. Walter Kaufmann. Trans. Walter Kaufmann and R. J. Hollingdale. New York: Vintage Books, 1969.

―――. *Thus Spoke Zarathustra: A Book for Everyone and No One*. Trans. R. J. Hollingdale. Middlesex: Penguin Books, 1961.

―――. *Twilight of the Idols* and *The Anti-Christ*. Trans. R. J. Hollingdale. New York: Penguin Books, 1985.

————. *The Will to Power*. Ed. Walter Kaufmann. Trans. Walter Kaufmann and R. J. Hollingdale. New York: Vintage Books, 1968.

Nozick, Robert. *Anarchy, State, and Utopia*. New York: Basic Books, 1974.

Nussbaum, Martha C. *The Fragility of Goodness: Luck and Ethics in Greek Tragedy and Philosophy*. Cambridge: Cambridge University Press, 1986.

O'Neill, John, ed. *On Critical Theory*. New York: Seabury Press, 1976.

Palmer, Richard. E. *Hermeneutics: Interpretation Theory in Schleiermacher, Dilthey, Heidegger, and Gadamer*. Evanston: Northwestern University Press, 1969.

Poster, Mark. *Foucault, Marxism and History*. Cambridge: Polity Press, 1984.

Rabinow, Paul, ed. *The Foucault Reader*. New York: Pantheon Books, 1984.

Rabinow, Paul and William M. Sullivan, eds. *Interpretive Social Science: A Second Look*. Los Angeles: University of California Press, 1987.

Rasmussen, David M. *Reading Habermas*. Cambridge: Basil Blackwell, 1990.

————, ed. *Universalism vs. Communitarianism: Contemporary Debates in Ethics*. Cambridge: MIT Press, 1990.

Rawls, John. *Political Liberalism*. New York: Columbia University Press, 1996.

————. *A Theory of Justice*. Cambridge: Harvard University Press, 1971.

Raz, Joseph. *The Morality of Freedom*. Oxford: Clarendon Press, 1986.

Ricoeur, Paul. *The Conflict of Interpretations: Essays in Hermeneutics*. Ed. Don Ihde. Evanston: Northwestern University Press, 1974.

————. "Ethics and Culture: Habermas and Gadamer in Dialogue." *Philosophy Today* 17.

————. *Freud and Philosophy: An Essay on Interpretation*. Trans. Denis Savage. New Haven: Yale University Press, 1970.

————. *From Text to Action: Essays in Hermeneutics II*. Trans. Kathleen Blamey and John Thompson. Evanston: Northwestern University Press, 1991.

—————. *Hermeneutics and the Human Sciences: Essays on Language, Action and Interpretation*. Ed. and trans. John B. Thompson. Cambridge: Cambridge University Press, 1981.

—————. "History as Narrative and Practice." *Philosophy Today* 29.

—————. *The Just*. Trans. David Pellauer. Chicago: University of Chicago Press, 2000.

—————. *Lectures on Ideology and Utopia*. Ed. George H. Taylor. New York: Columbia University Press, 1986.

—————. *Main Trends in Philosophy*. New York: Holmes and Meier Publishers, 1979.

—————. *Oneself As Another*. Trans. Kathleen Blamey. Chicago: University of Chicago Press, 1992.

—————. *The Rule of Metaphor: Multi-Disciplinary Studies of the Creation of Meaning in Language*. Trans. Robert Czerny. Toronto: University of Toronto Press, 1977.

—————. *Time and Narrative*. Vol. 1. Trans. Kathleen McLaughlin and David Pellauer. Chicago: University of Chicago Press, 1984.

Rockmore, Tom. *Habermas on Historical Materialism*. Bloomington: Indiana University Press, 1989.

Rorty, Richard. *Consequences of Pragmatism*. Minneapolis: University of Minnesota Press, 1982.

—————. *Contingency, Irony, and Solidarity*. Cambridge: Cambridge University Press, 1989.

—————. *Philosophical Papers*, 2 vols. Cambridge: Cambridge University Press, 1991.

—————. *Philosophy and the Mirror of Nature*. Princeton: Princeton University Press, 1979.

—————. "Thugs and Theorists: A Reply to Bernstein." *Political Theory* 15, no. 4.

Rousseau, Jean-Jacques. *The Social Contract and the Discourses*. Trans. G. D. H. Cole. New York: Everyman's Library, 1993.

Sandel, Michael J. *Democracy's Discontent: America in Search of a Public Philosophy*. Cambridge: Harvard University Press, 1996.

—————. *Liberalism and the Limits of Justice*. Cambridge: Cambridge University Press, 1982.

Schrag, Calvin O. *Communicative Praxis and the Space of Subjectivity*. Bloomington: Indiana University Press, 1989.

―――. *The Resources of Rationality: A Response to the Postmodern Challenge*. Bloomington: Indiana University Press, 1992.

Schutte, Ofelia. *Beyond Nihilism: Nietzsche Without Masks*. Chicago: University of Chicago Press, 1984.

Scott, Charles E. *The Question of Ethics: Nietzsche, Foucault, Heidegger*. Bloomington: Indiana University Press, 1990.

Sedgwick, Peter R. Ed. *Nietzsche: A Critical Reader*. Cambridge: Blackwell, 1995.

Shapiro, Gary and Alan Sica, eds. *Hermeneutics: Questions and Prospects*. Amherst: University of Massachusetts Press, 1984.

Silverman, Hugh J. *Gadamer and Hermeneutics*. New York: Routledge, 1991.

Simpson, Evan. *Good Lives and Moral Education*. New York: Peter Lang Publishing, 1989.

―――. "Principles and Customs in Moral Philosophy." *Metaphilosophy* 24, nos. 1 & 2.

―――, ed. *Anti-Foundationalism and Practical Reasoning: Conversations Between Hermeneutics and Analysis*. Edmonton: Academic Printing and Publishing, 1987.

Simpson, Evan and Clarke, Stanley, eds. *Anti-Theory in Ethics and Moral Conservatism*. Albany: State University of New York Press, 1989.

Smart, Barry. *Foucault, Marxism and Critique*. New York: Routledge, 1983.

Smith, P. Christopher. *Hermeneutics and Human Finitude: Toward a Theory of Ethical Understanding*. New York: Fordham University Press, 1991.

Stout, Jeffrey. *Ethics After Babel: The Languages of Morals and Their Discontents*. Boston: Beacon Press, 1988.

Strong, Tracy B. *Friedrich Nietzsche and the Politics of Transfiguration*. Berkeley: University of California Press, 1988.

Sullivan, Robert R. *Political Hermeneutics: The Early Thinking of Hans-Georg Gadamer*. University Park: The Pennsylvania State University Press, 1989.

Taylor, Charles. *The Malaise of Modernity*. Concord: House of Anansi Press, 1991.

———. *Philosophy and the Human Sciences: Philosophical Papers 2*. Cambridge: Cambridge University Press, 1985.

———. *Sources of the Self: The Making of the Modern Identity*. Cambridge: Harvard University Press, 1989.

Theunissen, Michael. *The Other: Studies in the Social Ontology of Husserl, Heidegger, Sartre, and Buber*. Trans. Christopher Macann. Cambridge: MIT Press, 1986.

Thiele, Leslie Paul. *Friedrich Nietzsche and the Politics of the Soul: A Study of Heroic Individualism*. Princeton: Princeton University Press, 1990.

Thompson, John. *Critical Hermeneutics: A Study in the Thought of Paul Ricoeur and Jürgen Habermas*. Cambridge: Cambridge University Press, 1981.

Toulmin, Stephen. "The Construal of Reality: Criticism in Modern and Postmodern Science." In *The Politics of Interpretation*, edited by W. J. T. Mitchell. Chicago: University of Chicago Press, 1983.

Unger, Roberto Mangabeira. *Knowledge and Politics*. New York: The Free Press, 1975.

Wachterhauser, Brice R, ed. *Hermeneutics and Modern Philosophy*. Albany: State University of New York Press, 1986.

Walzer, Michael. *Spheres of Justice: A Defense of Pluralism and Equality*. New York: Basic Books, 1983.

Warnke, Georgia. *Gadamer: Hermeneutics, Tradition and Reason*. Stanford: Stanford University Press, 1987.

———. *Justice and Interpretation*. Cambridge: MIT Press, 1993.

White, Stephen K. "Habermas's Communicative Ethics and the Development of Moral Consciousness." *Philosophy and Social Criticism* 10, no. 2.

———. *The Recent Work of Jürgen Habermas: Reason, Justice and Modernity*. Cambridge: Cambridge University Press, 1988.

———, ed. *The Cambridge Companion to Habermas*. Cambridge: Cambridge University Press, 1995.

Williams, Bernard. *Ethics and the Limits of Philosophy*. Cambridge: Cambridge University Press, 1985.

Wittgenstein, Ludwig. *Philosophical Investigations*. Trans. G. E. M. Anscombe. Oxford: Basil Blackwell, 1953.

Yovel, Yirmiyahu. Ed. *Nietzsche as Affirmative Thinker*. Boston: Martinus Nijhoff Publishers, 1986.

INDEX

action, 3, 99, 107–10, 177n1
Adorno, Theodor, 70, 174n1
aestheticism, 64
algorithms, 121
altruism, 21, 39
ambiguity, 4, 17
amor fati, 24–25, 42
Anti-Christ, The (Nietzsche), 23
application, 119–23
aristocracy, 28, 30, 46
Aristotelians, 122–23
Aristotle, 4, 108–10, 118, 120, 124–25, 127, 134
art, 19, 23–24
authority, 46
autonomy, 22, 28–29, 69, 79, 99, 167–68

behavior, 47, 49, 100, 109
Being and Time (Heidegger), 99–100, 152
Bentham, Jeremy, 47
Beyond Good and Evil (Nietzsche), 37
biases. *See* prejudice
bureaucracy, 70

capitalism, 68
Chomsky, Noam, 79
Christianity, 20, 28, 33, 93, 116
Churchill, Winston, 182n8
Civilization and it Discontents (Freud), 76
class structure, 89, 112–13
cognition, 79–80
competence theory, 89–90
consciousness: and critical theory, 72; and deception, 112; and dogma, 167; falsifications of, 112; historical, 7, 39,

95; and language, 74–75; moral, 79, 102, 106, 113–14; of phenomena, 7; and tradition, 100–101
conservatism, 11, 98, 105
contractarians, 2
critical theory, 68–69, 72
criticism: definition of, 116; and ethics, 12; genealogical, 40; and genealogy, 65; immanent, 150; moral, 38–40; and narrative, 110; normative, 102; as partisan, 40; perspective of, 59; practice of, 41, 97, 106; social, 2, 40, 65, 68, 70
critique: action of, 107; facticity of, 98–105; and genealogy, 50–55, 93; immanent, 150; method of, 2, 13, 36, 50; and perspectivism, 35–42; of power, 17, 50; of science, 69–77; and tradition, 92, 106

deception, 112
deduction, 97, 124
democracy, 41, 70, 120, 141
deontology, 3–4
Dewey, John, 4, 125–27, 174n27
dialogue. *See also* language narrative, 11, 71, 141, 152–53
Dilthey, Wilhelm, 56, 74
Discipline and Punish: The Birth of the Prison (Foucault), 47, 50
discourse. *See* language
dogmatism, 39, 51, 63, 88–89, 94–95, 101, 167
domination, 173n8
Dreyfus, Hubert, 56, 173n8

205